Augustus Frederick Nightingale

A Hand-book of Requirements for Admission to the Colleges

of the United States

With Miscellaneus Addenda

Augustus Frederick Nightingale

A Hand-book of Requirements for Admission to the Colleges of the United States
With Miscellaneus Addenda

ISBN/EAN: 9783744764773

Printed in Europe, USA, Canada, Australia, Japan

Cover: Foto ©Paul-Georg Meister /pixelio.de

More available books at **www.hansebooks.com**

A

HAND-BOOK

OF

REQUIREMENTS FOR ADMISSION

TO THE

COLLEGES OF THE UNITED STATES,

WITH

MISCELLANEOUS ADDENDA,

FOR THE USE OF

HIGH SCHOOLS, ACADEMIES, AND OTHER COLLEGE-PREPARATORY INSTITUTIONS.

COMPILED AND ARRANGED BY

A. F. NIGHTINGALE, A. M.,

PRINCIPAL OF THE LAKE VIEW HIGH SCHOOL, RAVENSWOOD (NEAR CHICAGO), ILLINOIS.

NEW YORK:
D. APPLETON AND COMPANY,
549 AND 551 BROADWAY.
1879.

TO

ALL THE PUPILS, OF BOTH SEXES,

OF OUR

SECONDARY SCHOOLS,

TO THE AMBITIOUS AND THE INDIFFERENT,

𝔗𝔥𝔦𝔰 𝔅𝔬𝔬𝔨 𝔦𝔰 𝔍𝔫𝔰𝔠𝔯𝔦𝔟𝔢𝔡,

WITH THE HOPE THAT IT MAY LEND

AN INSPIRATION TO ALL, TO AIM TOWARD

THE ATTAINMENT OF THE IMPORTANT ENDS OF LIFE,

EDUCATION, CULTURE, SUCCESS, HAPPINESS.

ANNOUNCEMENT.

This Hand-book represents in the selection of colleges the maximum and minimum requirements for admission to any meritorious college in the United States.

In the selection of institutions, the aim has been, not to imply that those excluded do not rank equally high with many here mentioned, but to represent the different sections of the country, the leading denominational colleges, and a few of the most important State universities of the West.

An average of the requirements to enter the colleges represented in the book will admit a student to the Freshman class of any college or university not named—so that it becomes a chart of universal application to the colleges of the United States.

A thorough knowledge of the Latin and Greek Grammar, including prosody, is required to enter the classical course of any good college, and marked proficiency in the common English branches—especially grammar or language—is insisted upon for entrance to both classical and scientific courses. In addition to the two general courses, classical and scientific, most of the colleges have a Latin scientific course, for entrance to which French or German is substituted for Greek. The State universities and many of the others have, also, courses in Civil Engineering, Mining Engineering, and in Architecture and Design.

Most of the colleges now furnish, in the last two years of the classical and scientific courses, a wide range of polytechnic studies, from which students may generally select. Requirements for admission to any of the courses except classical, are generally the same as for admission to the scientific course.

A complete list of the colleges and universities of the United States is given, with miscellaneous addenda which will be of interest to all the patrons and friends of higher education.

INTRODUCTION.

SEVERAL motives suggested the compilation of this little book. When students wisely conclude to make a college education their ambition and aim, they very naturally send for one or a dozen college catalogues, to ascertain their requirements and other information which will enable them to decide what college to enter; but the great mass of facts which these catalogues contain often tends to confuse the mind, and to render of little avail the trouble occasioned and expense incurred.

To obviate these difficulties, to present a concise and yet authentic table of requirements for admission to the leading colleges of the United States, and to give other information which will be of value and interest to all the students of our secondary schools, has been one purpose in the preparation of this hand-book.

The arrangement in parallel columns of the requirements for admission to the classical and scientific courses of the forty-four colleges mentioned will, we hope, furnish a convenient chart for reference and comparison.

These facts have been gathered with great care from the latest catalogues and circulars of these institutions; and where these facts have been in any way involved or deficient, correspondence has been elicited from the college presidents, who have invariably answered all inquiries, so that we feel assured that the book may be taken as a safe guide in determining the amount and nature of the work required in preparation.

Catalogues of several years have been consulted; very slight changes are made from year to year; and, while the requirements are taken from the official reports of the current year, students will find it safe to follow them for several years to come.

Another motive has been to impress upon the minds of the pupils of secondary schools the absolute importance of a thorough preparation. *Quality rather than quantity is the pressing demand of all the colleges;* and, while pupils are expected to read all that is required in the classics, and to acquaint themselves with all that is demanded in mathematics and English, *conditions and rejections are based upon poor quality rather than insufficient quantity in preparation.*

Incompetency in instruction and the haste which makes waste so common among students are deplorably conspicuous in our preparatory schools, and we would reiterate the thought that, if students would render the instruction and opportunities of their college life profitable and pleasant, they will leave no means unemployed to secure the best instruction in their preparatory work, even if they add a year to their preparation, or neglect some portion of the amount required. We have appended the questions which were used at the entrance examination for the current year at Yale, Bowdoin, Dartmouth, and Boston University. They present a fair outline of what is required by all the colleges, and may be studied to advantage by preparatory pupils.

We have purposely omitted any tabulated statement of the expenses necessarily incurred in obtaining a college education, for many reasons :

First, the catalogues do not give such information on this subject as will constitute any adequate guide to the student ; secondly, tuition for indigent and meritorious students *is practically free* in most of the colleges, and those who are compelled to pay are generally sufficiently able not to make this an item in their decision ; thirdly, the disposition of the student and the restrained or loose indulgence of parents are the real factors which enter into a proper computation of the economical or extravagant expenditures of college life.

The cost of books and the price of board are the real items of college expense, and these do not differ materially in any of the best colleges. Any student can honorably and comfortably take a four years' course *away from home,* at an annual expense, covering all essential items, of four hundred dollars. Many can and do curtail their expenses within much narrower limits, and it ought to cost no one, in any college, who would profit by the advantages offered, more than six hundred dollars a year.

The statistics regarding the "Enumeration of Students," "Latin Pronunciation in Use," "Harvard Examinations for Women," indeed all the statistics, have been arranged with great care and scrupulous accuracy.

In presenting this book to the public, the compiler would render his grateful acknowledgments to the college presidents, Latin professors, and to all the officers consulted, for their generous promptness and repeated courtesies in answering letters, in furnishing statistics, and in rendering every facility to aid in making the book, what we hope it may prove, of interest and value to the teachers and students of all our secondary schools.

A. F. N.

CHICAGO, *January, 1879.*

COLLEGE REQUIREMENTS.

NAME OF COLLEGE, OR UNIVERSITY.	Course.	LATIN.				GREEK, OR MODERN LANGUAGES.		
		Com. of Cæsar, No. of Books.	Virgil.	Orations of Cicero.	Latin Prose.	Books Anabasis.	Books Homer.	Greek Prose.
Amherst College (Congregational), *Amherst, Massachusetts.* Established 1821.	Classical.	Four; also translation of easy Latin at sight.[1]	Bucolics, two Georgics, six of Æneid.	Seven, including the Manilian Law.	First two parts Harkness, or equivalent.	Four.	Three.	First twenty exercises, Jones's.
	Scientific.	Four.	Six of Æneid.	Seven.	First two parts Harkness, or equivalent.	Otto's French, Part I.		
Boston University (Methodist), *Boston, Massachusetts.* Both Sexes. Established 1871.	All courses.	Four.[1]	Bucolics, and six of Æneid.	Seven.	First two parts Harkness, or equivalent.	Four.	Three.	Simple sentences, White's First Lessons, sixty.
	Requirements in 1881.	Four, and Sallust's Catiline.	Bucolics, and nine of Æneid; Latin at sight.	Eight, and Cato Major.	First two parts Harkness, or equivalent.	Four.	Three, and first book Herodotus.	Simple sentences, Jones's Greek Lessons.
Bowdoin College (Congregational), *Brunswick, Maine.* Established 1802.	Classical.	Four, or Sallust.[2]	Bucolics, Georgics, and six of Æneid.	Seven.	Allen's, thirty-five lessons, or equivalent.	Four.	Two.	Jones's.
	Scientific.	Four, or Sallust.	Bucolics, Georgics, six of Æneid.	Seven.	Allen's, thirty-five lessons, or equivalent.			
Brown University (Baptist), *Providence, Rhode Island.* Established 1764.	Classical.	Five.[1]	Bucolics, Georgics, six of Æneid.	Eight.	First two parts Harkness, or equivalent.	Five.	Two books Homer's Odyssey.	First twenty exercises, Arnold's.
	Scientific.	Five, or equiv.				Otto's French, thirty-seven chapters, or equivalent.		
California State University (Non-sectarian), *Oakland, California.* Both Sexes. Established 1855.	Classical.	Four.[2]	Six of Æneid, Georgics, Eclogues.	Six.	Allen's, twenty-six lessons.	Four.	Two.	Jones's.
	Scientific.	[3]						

[1] English pronunciation in Latin.   [2] Roman pronunciation in Latin.
[3] No requirements in Latin or Natural Sciences are insisted upon, but candidates are earnestly recommended to pursue the study of Latin one year, and also that of local Botany, Mineralogy, and Natural History, before entering; also one of the Modern Languages.

	MATHEMATICS.		MISCELLANEOUS.	GENERAL REMARKS.
Algebra.	Geometry.	Trigonometry.		
Loomis's, to Quad.	Simple Proportions, no Areas, four of Loomis.		Common English, including Metric System, Tozer's Classical Geography, Otto's French, Part I.	**Admits** students at fifteen. In Scientific course, modern languages **are** substituted for Greek, and Latin is omitted after the Freshman year. Gymnasium exercise compulsory. Long list of prizes. Students may also pursue a partial **course**, obtaining a certificate **but not a degree.**
Loomis's, to Quad.	Simple Proportions, no Areas, four of Loomis.		Common English, including Metric System, Tozer's Classical Geography.	
To Quad.	Simple Proportions, no Areas, four of Loomis.		Common English, including Metric System, General History (Freeman), English History (Berard), Ancient History and Geography, Smith's Manuals, Hart's Rhetoric, easy French.	Sustains schools of Law, Medicine, Theology, Music, Oratory, and Post-Graduate courses. In '79, Appletons' Science Primers or equivalent in Chemistry and Physics, and Loomis's Alg. comp. required. In '80, Sallust's Catiline, Cato Major, eight orations of Cicero; also, easy German and Plane and Solid Geometry entire. *All these*, in addition to *Chart* requirements. **There are two** examinations: **one preliminary, one** final. May be one year apart, each covering about one-half of requirements.
Univ. Alg. complete.	Plane and Solid entire.		Common English,[4] including Metric System and theory of Logarithms, Hart's Rhetoric, Chemistry (Roscoe's Primer), Elements of Physics (Stewart's Primer), French and German, translation at sight of easy prose, English and General History, Ancient History and Geography.	
Loomis's, through Quad.	Loomis, Books 1 and 3.		Arithmetic, English Grammar, Geography, Ancient and Modern.	**Sustains** school of Medicine and Post-Graduate course. Maintains several prizes. Students are required to elect between gymnastics and military exercises.
Loomis's, through Quad.	Loomis, Books 1 and 3.		Arithmetic, English Grammar, Geography, Descriptive and Physical.	
Through Quad.	Plane and Solid.		Common English, including Metric System, Craik's English of Shakespeare, Cæsar, Act I., Otto's French, thirty-seven chapters.	Sustains Post - Graduate course. Students may pass a preliminary examination one year in advance in Greek Grammar and Reader and three books of Anabasis; also, Latin Grammar, Cæsar and Cicero, or Cæsar and six books of Æneid; also in Arithmetic; but in no other branches. Several prizes; 625 scholarships of $1,000 each; income given to aid meritorious students. College rents Gymnasium for exclusive use of students.
Through Quad.	Plane and Solid.		Common English, including Metric System, exercises in English Composition, Craik's English of Shakespeare, Julius Cæsar, Act I.	
To Quad.	Four books of Legendre.		Common English, including Metric System, Physical Geography, Hart's Composition and Rhetoric.	Admits students at sixteen. Sustains Post-Graduate course. For the Literary course, Latin Grammar and Reader and four books of Cæsar are required, in addition to requirements for Scientific course; also colleges of Agriculture, Mechanics, Mining, Engineering, Chemistry, Medicine, Pharmacy, Military Tactics. Law School just established.
To Quad.	Four books of Legendre, or Loomis's.		Common English, including Metric System, Physical Geography, Hart's Composition and Rhetoric.	

[4] Also a brief essay on some theme to be announced at the time of the examination.

NAME OF COLLEGE, OR UNIVERSITY.	Course.	LATIN.				GREEK, OR MODERN LANGUAGES.		
		Com. of Caesar, No. of Books.	Virgil.	Orations of Cicero.	Latin Prose.	Books Anabasis.	Books Homer.	Greek Prose.
Chicago University (Baptist), *Chicago, Illinois.* Both Sexes. Established 1859.	Classical.	Four.[5]	Six of Æneid.	Seven.	First two parts Harkness, or equivalent.	Three.	Odyssey from Boise and Freeman's Selections.	Jones's.
	Scientific.	6						
Colby University (Baptist), *Waterville, Maine.* Both Sexes. Established 1819.	Classical (all courses).	Four, and Sallust's Catiline.[7]	Six of Æneid.	Six, including Manilian Law.	First two parts Harkness, or equivalent.	Three, or equivalent.		Jones's, twelve exercises.
Columbia College (Episcopal), *New York, New York.* Established 1754.	Classical (all courses).[4]	All.[5]	Six of Æneid.	Six.	First two parts Harkness, or equivalent.	Four.	Three.	Arnold's.
Cornell University (Non-sectarian), *Ithaca, New York.* Both Sexes. Established 1865.	Classical.	Four.[5]	Six of Æneid, Bucolics.	Eight.	First twelve chapters Arnold.	Four.	Three.	Arnold's.
	Scientific.					Otto's French Grammar, Voltaire, three books Charles XII., or equivalent; or German, with seventy-five pages Whit. Reader, or equivalent.		
Cornell College (Methodist), *Mount Vernon, Iowa.* Both Sexes. Established 1851.	Classical.	Four.[5]		Six.	Harkness, one part.	Two.		Simple exercises.
	Scientific.	Four.		Six.	Harkness, one part.	French Grammar and Reader, one hundred pages translation.		
Dartmouth College (Congregational), *Hanover, New Hampshire.* Established 1769.	Classical.	Four.[7]	Georgics, Six of Æneid.	Six.	Abbott's.	Four.	Two.	First twenty exercises, Jones.
	Scientific.							
Hamilton College (Presbyterian), *Clinton, New York.* Established 1812.	Classical (all courses).	Four, and Sallust's Catiline.[7]	Six of Æneid, Eclogues.	Eight.	Arnold, twelve chapters, or equivalent.	Two.	Two.	

* Roman pronunciation in Latin.   4 *See* General Remarks for Philosophical Course.   7 English pronunciation in Latin.
5 For admission to the School of Mines, Arithmetic, including Metric System, five chapters of Peck's Manual of Algebra, five books of Davies's Legendre, twenty-five lessons of Jewett's Ollendorff's French Grammar, and twenty lessons of Otto's German Grammar, are required.

COLLEGES OF THE UNITED STATES.

MATHEMATICS.			MISCELLANEOUS.	GENERAL REMARKS.
Algebra.	Geometry.	Trigonometry.		
Loomis's, to Chapter XVIII.	First six books.		Common English, including Metric System, Elements of Natural Philosophy, Freeman's Outlines of History.	Sustains schools of Law, Medicine, and Theology. For the Philosophical course, four books of Cæsar and four orations of Cicero are added to the requirements of the Scientific course.
Loomis's, to Chapter XVIII.	First six books.		Common English, including Metric System, Elements Natural Philosophy, Freeman's Outlines of History, Physical Geography.	
Through Quad., Olney's complete.	Olney's, Part II., seven sections Plane.		Arithmetic, English Grammar, Geography, Ancient and Modern. (Pupils are urged to read attentively some manual of Greek and Roman History.)	Maintains a large number of scholarships for meritorious students; also several prizes. Gymnasium, exercise voluntary. Pupils are allowed to take a partial course, and receive certificates for success attained.
To Quadratics.	Simple Proportions. No Areas, Four of Davies's Legendre.		Common English, including Metric System, Ancient Geography.*	Several prizes maintained and special courses of study. A number of free scholarships. Free tuition to meritorious pupils.
Through Quad., including Radicals.	All Plane.		Physiology, Huxley and Youmans, Physical Geography, Grecian History, Smith's, Common English, including Metric System.	There are also courses in Literature and Philosophy, both of which require Latin, but not Greek, for admission. There are, also, departments of Agriculture, Architecture, Civil Engineering, Military Science, and schools of special studies besides, and an extended Post-Graduate course. Ladies must be seventeen years of age, for admission. Over five hundred students.
University complete.	Plane and Solid.	Plane and Spherical.	Common English, including Metric System, Physiology, and Physical Geography.	
Through Quad.	Four.		Common English.	Military drill required, unless students are specially excused.
Through Quad.	Four.		Common English.	
To Quad., Olney's University.	Olney's Plane.		Common English, including Metric System, Ancient Geography, English History.	Maintains an Agricultural and Medical Department. Also, Thayer School of Civil Engineering, especially for Post-Graduates. Several prizes in regular college courses. Pupils are admitted on diplomas of college preparatory institutions, and are then on probation for three months.
Olney's School Algebra complete.	Plane.		Common English, including Metric System, Physical Geography, Physiology, Book-keeping.	
To Quad.	All Plane.		Common English, including Metric System, Ancient Geography, Grecian and Roman Antiquities.	Sustains a Law Department. Several prizes in college courses. Whole number of graduates to 1878—2,085.

* First seventeen pages of Schmidt's "Course of Ancient Geography." Students will be required to name the principal towns of Greece; also upon page 90, et seq., of the same work, to "Upper Italy," page 102, and to state the principal towns of Italy and Sicily; and farther, upon "Asia Minor," page 191, et seq., Mysia, and the principal rivers, mountains, and towns of Asia Minor.

NAME OF COLLEGE, OR UNIVERSITY.	Course.	LATIN.				GREEK, OR MODERN LANGUAGES.		
		Com. of Cæsar, No. of Books.	Virgil.	Orations of Cicero.	Latin Prose.	Books Anabasis.	Books Homer.	Greek Prose.
Harvard College (Non-sectarian). *Cambridge, Massachusetts.* Established 1638.	Course I.[10]	All. 11 12	All of Æneid.	Ten.	Harkness or Arnold's.	All.	Three.	Arnold's.
	Course II.	Two.	Six of Æneid.	Eight, or six and Cato Major.	Harkness or Arnold's.	Four.	Two.	Arnold's.
Illinois Industrial University (Non-sectarian), *Urbana, Illinois.* Both Sexes. Established 1868.	Classical,	Four.[13]	Six of Æneid.	Six.	First two parts Harkness, or Arnold's, to Pas. Voice.	Four.		Arnold's or Jones's.
	English and Modern Languages,	Four.	Six of Æneid.		First two parts Harkness, or Arnold's, to Pas. Voice.			
Indiana Asbury University (Methodist), *Greencastle, Indiana.* Both Sexes. Established 1837.	Classical.	Two.	Two of Æneid.		Harkness two parts.	Two.		Jones's.
	Philosophical.	Two.[12]	Two of Æneid.		Harkness two parts.			
Iowa State University (Non-sectarian), *Iowa City, Iowa.* Both Sexes. Established 1860.	Classical,	Two.[14]	Six of Æneid.	Four.	Allen and Greenough, or equivalent.	Ahn's German, with Adler's Reader.		
	Scientific.					Ahn's German, with Adler's Reader.		
Johns Hopkins University, *Baltimore, Maryland.* Established 1876.	Classical,	Four. Also Ovid, 2,500 verses.12	Five of Æneid, Eclogues, also Livy, Book 21.	Seven, also Horace, Odes, Books 1 and 2.	Harkness, or equivalent.	Three, also Herodotus, Book 8.	Three, also Euripides's Medea, or any one play.	Jones's.
	Scientific.	Four. Also Ovid, 2,500 verses.	Five of Æneid, Eclogues, also Livy, Book 21.	Seven, also Horace, Odes, Books 1 and 2.	Harkness, or equivalent.	Proficiency in French and German, including thorough acquaintance with Grammar. Ability to read and write these languages.		

10 These two courses are called **Method II.** Method I. prescribes **a minimum requisition in every study, and a maximum in two,** to be selected from the four following principal studies, Latin, **Greek, Mathematics, Physical** and **Natural Science.** Method I. will be used exclusively in 1880 and thereafter, as follows: Minimum in **Latin—Cæsar, four books;** Virgil, **four of Æneid,** and Eclogues; Easy Latin at sight; Latin Prose. Maximum—Virgil's Æneid, Books V.-IX.; Cicero's Orations against **Catiline;** average passages from Cicero's Orations at sight. Minimum in Greek—Anabasis, four books; **Iliad, two books;** White's **Lessons in Greek,** fifty-one lessons. Maximum—Herodotus in Goodwin (pages 112-151), and Iliad, **Books III., IV., and VI.** Minimum in Mathematics—As in Course I. Maximum—Logarithms and Plane Trigonometry, and Solid **Geometry.** Minimum in Science—Rolfe's and Gillette's Natural Philosophy, **or** first two parts of Arnott's Physics. Maximum—Arnott's **Physics to Part** IV., **Sec.** III., and either Eliot and

MATHEMATICS.			MISCELLANEOUS.	GENERAL REMARKS.
Algebra.	Geometry.	Trigonometry.		
Through Quad. and Logs.	All Plane or thirteen chapters Pierce.		Common English, including Metric System, Ancient History (Smith's Smaller) and Geography, Physical Geography and Science,[b] French or German.	Departments of Law, Theology, and Medicine, and Post-Graduate courses; also Schools of Dentistry and Agriculture, Teachers' courses in Lawrence Scientific School, and elective courses of study. There may be two examinations for admission, one year apart, but at the preliminary examination students must pass in at least five subjects entire. More than 1,300 students.
All.	Plane and Solid. Also Elements of Plane Analytical Geometry.	Six chapters Pierce, or eight chap. Chauvenet, large print.	Common English, including Metric System, Ancient History and Geography, Physical Geography and Science, French or German, easy translations.	
Through Quad.	Plane and Solid.		Common English, including Metric System and Word Analysis, Elements of English Composition.	Maintains four colleges, namely, Agriculture, Natural Science, Literature and Science, Engineering, in each of which are several Schools or Departments. There are also Schools of "Military Science," "Domestic Science," and Art. It is eminently a Polytechnic Institution.
Through Quad.	Plane and Solid.		Common English, including Metric System and Word Analysis, Dalton's Physiology, Elements of English Composition, Botany, Peck's Ganot's Philosophy.	
Olney's complete.			Common English, including Metric System, Physical Geography, Book-keeping, Geography of Heavens, Physiology, Drawing, Natural History, Elements of Natural Philosophy.	Admits students at fourteen. Maintains a Theological and Normal course. Military drill required the first two years; optional, last two. Several prizes.
Olney's complete.			Common English, including Metric System, Physical Geography, Book-keeping, Geography of Heavens, Physiology, Drawing, Natural History, Elements of Natural Philosophy.	
Ficklin's University.	Two books Robinson.		Common English, Hart's Composition and Rhetoric, Dalton's Physiology, Elements of Astronomy.	Maintains Departments of Law, Medicine, and Civil Engineering. Students must be sixteen. Several prizes awarded. Greek commenced with Freshman year.
Ficklin's University.	Two books Robinson.		Common English, Hart's Composition and Rhetoric, Dalton's Physiology, Elements of Astronomy, Chemistry, Physics, and Mineralogy.	
Todhunter, chapters 1–38.	Chauvenet's, nine books, also minimum course of Howison's Analytical.	Chauvenet's, eight chapters, also use of Logs.	Common English, including Metric System, Ancient History and Geography, Greek and Roman Antiquities; also one of the following: Botany, Natural Philosophy, Physical Geography.	Maintains extended courses of instruction beyond the regular College course. Numerous lecture courses in Classics and Sciences. Unusual facilities for Laboratory practice. Several scholarships. Four examinations—preliminary, matriculation, baccalaureate, final. It is eminently a Post-Graduate Institution.
Todhunter, chapters 1–38.	Chauvenet's, nine books, also minimum course of Howison's Analytical.	Chauvenet's, eight chapters, also use of Logs.	Common English, including Metric System, Ancient History and Geography, Greek and Roman Antiquities; also one of the following: Botany, Natural Philosophy, Physical Geography.	

Storer's Chemistry, or Botany (Gray's "How Plants Grow"); English and French, or German, as in "Miscellaneous." Candidates should have a thorough acquaintance with English Literature.
[b] Sallust's Catiline, 4,000 lines of Ovid, and Cato Major, are preferred in place of two books of Cæsar, two Orations of Cicero, and the last five books of the Æneid.
[13] Roman pronunciation.   [14] English pronunciation.
[15] In Physical Science, pupils should prepare in Gray's "How Plants Grow," with analysis of simple specimens, or Balfour Stewart's "Primer of Physics," with knowledge of simple experiments, or Rolfe and Gillet's "Handbook of the Stars" (124 pages), or Roscoe's "Primer of Chemistry."

NAME OF COLLEGE, OR UNIVERSITY.	Course.	LATIN.				GREEK, OR MODERN LANGUAGES.		
		Com. of Cæsar, No. of Books.	Virgil.	Orations of Cicero.	Latin Prose.	Books Anabasis.	Books Homer.	Greek Prose.
Kenyon College (Episcopalian), *Gambier, Ohio.* Established 1824.	Classical (all courses).	Three.[16]	Four of Æneid.	Four.	Arnold, seven chapters.	Three.	One.	Simple exercises.
Lafayette College (Presbyterian), *Easton, Pennsylvania.* Established 1832.	Classical.	Four.[16]	Six of Æneid, and Bucolics.	Seven.	Harkness, Part I.	All.	None but Gospels in Greek Testament, except Mark.	Arnold's twenty sections, or Jones's twelve lessons.
	Scientific.	Four (optional).	Six of Æneid, Bucolics (optional).	Seven (optional).	Harkness, Part I. (optional).			
Meadville, or Allegheny College (Methodist), *Meadville, Pennsylvania.* Both Sexes. Established 1815.	Classical (all courses).	Four, or Sallust's Catiline.[17]	Six of Æneid, and Bucolics.	Eight.	Harkness, two parts, or equivalent.	Four books Anabasis, and Goodwin's Reader, or six terms French or German.		
Michigan State University (Non-sectarian), *Ann Arbor, Michigan.* Both Sexes. Established 1841.	Classical.	Four.[18]	All of Æneid.	Six.	First two parts Harkness, or Arnold, forty-four exercises.	Three.		Jones's, or Arnold's.
	Scientific.	[18]				Otto's Grammar, with seventy-five pages Bocher's Otto's French Reader.		
Middlebury College (Congregational), *Middlebury, Vermont.* Established 1797.	Classical (all courses).	Four.[17]	Six of Æneid, and Bucolics.	Six.	Arnold's, six chapters.	Three.	Two.	Jones's twelve lessons.
Minnesota State University (Non-sectarian), *St. Anthony, Minnesota.* Both Sexes. Established 1868.	Classical.	Three.[17]	Four of Æneid.	Four.		Three.		
	Scientific.							

[16] English pronunciation.   [17] Roman pronunciation.
[18] One year's study of Latin will be required for admission to the course on and after September, 1879. Jones's First Latin Book, or Harkness's Latin Reader.

MATHEMATICS.			MISCELLANEOUS.	GENERAL REMARKS.
Algebra.	Geometry.	Trigonometry.		
To Quad.	Tappan's, to and including theory of Parallel Lines.		Common English, including Metric System, Ancient Geography, Liddell's History of Rome, twenty-four chapters, Smith's History of Greece to page 102; Baird's Classical Manual is also recommended.	Maintains a Theological course.
To Quad.	Plane, two books.		Arithmetic, Metric System, Geography, Ancient and Modern.	Maintains special courses in Civil Engineering and Chemistry, Mining Engineering, and Metallurgy; also, a Post-Graduate course. Awards several prizes. Has a Law Department, which embraces two years of study.
Through Quadrat's.	Plane, two books.		Common English, Metric System, Elements of Natural Philosophy, Outlines of History, general contents of Bible.	
Algebra complete.	Three books.		Arithmetic, English Grammar, Orthography, general facts of History, Physiology, Elements of Natural Philosophy and Botany.	Students admitted at fifteen. School of Military Science recently established. In Scientific course, French and German take the place of much of the Greek and Latin of the Classical course. There is a course of Latin and Modern Languages, which omits Greek entirely.
Olney's, complete, to Appendix.	Plane, Solid, Spherical, or Olney, two parts.		Common English,[19] including Metric System, Hart's Rhetoric, Ancient Geography (Italy, Greece, and Asia Minor), Grecian and Roman History (Smith's).	Maintains course in Civil Engineering, Mining Engineering, Architecture, and Design; also, Departments of Law, Medicine, and Surgery (including Homœopathic College); a College of Dentistry, School of Pharmacy; also, a Post-Graduate course. Another course, which shall be the natural sequel of the so-called English Course of High Schools, has recently been established. No languages are required, but a thorough knowledge of English, Mathematics, and Sciences. Over eleven hundred students.
Olney's, complete, to Appendix.	Plane, Spherical, Solid, or Olney, two parts.		Common English, including Metric System, General History (Anderson), Natural Philosophy, Gray's Botany, twenty-seven chapters, Shaw's English Literature, Geometrical Drawing, Huxley and Youmans's Physiology.	
Through Quad.	Three books Loomis.		Arithmetic, Ancient History, and Geography.	Maintains several prizes and scholarships.
To Theory of Equations.	Plane.		Common English, Outlines of General History, English Composition and Rhetoric, Gray's Botany, Ancient History and Geography, Elements of Geology.	Admits students at fourteen. Maintains Colleges of Agriculture and Mechanical Arts, with those of Law and Medicine proposed. Military exercise required in Collegiate Department.
To Theory of Equations.	Plane.		Common English, Outlines of General History, Gray's Botany, English Composition and Rhetoric, Physical Geography, Natural Philosophy, Elementary Astronomy, English History, Higher English Analysis, Physiology, Elements of Geology, Free-hand and Geometrical Drawing.	

[19] In English Language, each candidate will be required to write not less than two pages (foolscap), correct in spelling, punctuation, grammar, etc., on a subject assigned at time of examination.

2

NAME OF COLLEGE, OR UNIVERSITY.	Course.	LATIN.				GREEK, OR MODERN LANGUAGES.		
		Com. of Cæsar, No. of Books.	Virgil.	Orations of Cicero.	Latin Prose.	Books Anabasis.	Books Homer.	Greek Prose.
Northwestern University (Methodist), *Evanston, Illinois.* Both Sexes. Established 1855.	Classical.	Four.[20]	Eight of Æneid.	Seven.	First two parts Harkness, or equivalent.	Three.	Three.	Jones's.
	Scientific.							
Notre Dame University (Roman Catholic), *Notre Dame, Indiana.* Established 1842.	Classical.	Two.[21]	Nepos, five lives, instead of Virgil.	St. Jerome Hilarionis Vita, instead of Cicero.	Arnold, fifty exercises.	Three.		Simple exercises.
	Scientific.				A good knowledge of German or French.			
Oberlin College (Congregational), *Oberlin, Ohio.* Both Sexes. Established 1833.	Classical and Scientific.	One. Also Sal.'s Catil.[22]	Five.	Four.	First two parts Harkness, or equivalent.	Three.	Two.	
	Literary.		Latin Grammar. Latin Reader.		First part Harkness, or equivalent.			
Princeton, or College of New Jersey (Presbyterian), *Princeton, New Jersey.* Established 1746.	Classical.	Five. Also Sal.'s Catil. or Jugurtha.[22]	Six of Æneid.	Six.	First twelve chapters Arnold.	Three.	Two.	First thirty exercises of Arnold.
	Scientific.	Three.	Two of Æneid.					
Rensselaer Polytechnic Institute (Non-sectarian), *Troy, New York.* Established 1824.	Civil Engineering.							

[20] English pronunciation. [21] Both English and Continental pronunciation in use. [22] Roman pronunciation.

MATHEMATICS			MISCELLANEOUS.	GENERAL REMARKS.
Algebra.	Geometry.	Trigonometry.		
Through Quad.	Plane.		Common English, including Metric System, Ancient History and Geography, Natural Philosophy.	Maintains Colleges of Law, Music, Medicine, and Theology;[*] also, courses in Civil Engineering, Modern Languages, and Art. Has a Stock-Company Gymnasium. A large number of prizes awarded. Very extensive library. Over four hundred students, exclusive of Preparatory and Theological Departments.
Through Quad.	Plane.		Common English, including Metric System, Elements of Natural Philosophy and Physiology.	
Robinson's University to Series.	Plane.		Common English, including Metric System, Roman History.	Maintains a Law Department; also in Civil Engineering, Commercial and Post-Graduate courses. Gold Medals are awarded for proficiency; also many other prizes.
Robinson's University to Simple Equations.			Common English, including Metric System.	
Olney's, complete, or equivalent.	Plane.		Common English, including Metric System, Ancient History, Alden's Science of Government.	Maintains a Theological course; also, Conservatory of Music. About six hundred students, exclusive of Preparatory Department; eleven hundred in all.
Olney's, complete, or equivalent.			Common English, including Metric System.	
Through Quad. of one unknown quantity.	First book Euclid, or equivalent.		Common English, including Metric System, Ancient Geography.	Scientific course includes Civil Engineering and Architecture. Several prizes and scholarships maintained; also, fellowships for Post-Graduates. No secret societies allowed. Biennial examinations in College Department. Gymnasium, including billiards. Nearly five hundred students.
Through Quad. of one unknown quantity.	First book Euclid, or equivalent.		Common English, including Metric System.	
Through Quad.	Davies's Legendre, five books.		Higher Arithmetic, including Metric System, English Grammar (including Spelling), and Geography.	This institution, although maintaining but one course of study, offers special advantages to students desiring discipline in mathematics, and Physical and Natural Sciences. Graduates number about six hundred.

[*] The Theological School is called the "Garrett Biblical Institute," and is a corporate institution, entirely distinct from the University.

NAME OF COLLEGE, OR UNIVERSITY.	Course.	Com. of Caesar. No. of Books.	Virgil.	Orations of Cicero.	Latin Prose.	Books Anabasis.	Books Homer.	Greek Prose.
					LATIN.		GREEK, OR MODERN LANGUAGES.	
Rochester University (Baptist), *Rochester, New York.* Established 1850.	Classical.	Four.[14]	Six of Æneid.	Four, including Poet Archias, and Manilian Law.	Harkness's Part II., or Arnold's to Passive Voice, or equivalent.	Three.	One.	
	Scientific.	Four.	Six of Æneid.	Four, as above.	Harkness's Part II., or Arnold's to Passive Voice, or equivalent.			
Simpson Centenary College (Methodist), *Indianola, Iowa.* Both Sexes. Established 1866.	Classical.	Two.[25]	Six of Æneid.		First two parts Harkness.	Three.		Jones's.
	Scientific.							
Smith College (Non-sectarian), *Northampton, Massachusetts.* Woman's. Established 1875.	Classical (all courses).	Four, or Sallust's Catil.[23]	Six of Æneid.	Seven.	First thirty exercises Arnold's.	Three.	Two.	First eighteen exercises, Jones's.
Syracuse University (Methodist), *Syracuse, New York.* Both Sexes. Established 1872.	Classical.	Four, Also, Sal.'s Catil.[26]	Six of Æneid.	Four.	First two parts Harkness, or Allen and Greenough's Part I., complete.	Three.	Two.	
	Scientific.	Four, or equiv.						
Trinity College (Episcopalian), *Hartford, Connecticut.* Established 1823.	Classical (all courses).	Six.[25]	Six of Æneid, Eclogues, and one of Georgics.	Seven, including Manilian law.	Twelve chapters of Arnold.	Five.	Two.	Arnold to Section Twelve.
Tufts College (Universalist), *College Hill, Massachusetts.* Established 1855.	Classical.	Four. Also, Andr.' Ovid's Metamorphoses.[22]	Six of Æneid.	Seven, including Manilian Law.	First two parts Harkness, or equivalent.	Four.	Three.	Simple exercises.
	Philosophic.	Four. Also, Andr.' Ovid's Metamorphoses.	Six of Æneid.	Seven, including Manilian Law.	First two parts Harkness, or equivalent.	Otto's French Grammar entire. Six books Télémaque.		

[24] English and Continental.   [23] English pronunciation.   [26] Both English and Roman pronunciation in use.

MATHEMATICS.			MISCELLANEOUS.	GENERAL REMARKS.
Algebra.	Geometry.	Trigonometry.		
To Quad., Robinson's University.	Six books Robinson.		Common English, including Metric System, Gilmore's Art of Expression.	Maintains an Eclectic course for students not candidates for a degree. Maintains several prizes and scholarships, including Post-Graduate Scholarships.
To Quad., Robinson's University.	Six books Robinson.		Common English, including Metric System, Gilmore's Art of Expression.	
To Quad.	Plane.		Common English, including Metric System, Composition and Rhetoric, and Natural Philosophy.	Maintains a Law Department (located at Des Moines); also, Eclectic and Commercial courses of study.
To Quad.	Plane.		Common English, including Metric System, Composition and Rhetoric, and Natural Philosophy.	
Through Quad.	Two books.		Common English, including Metric System.	Greek required for admission. A Literary course, with special attention to Modern Languages, especially English, and a Scientific course, with special attention to Mathematics and Natural Sciences, are maintained, besides the Classical course, but requirements are the same to all. High-school graduates may take a special course of from one to four years.
Robinson's University to Quad., including Radicals.	Plane, Davies's Legendre. five books.		Common English, including Metric System, Ancient History, Smith's Greece, fourteen chapters; Merivale's Rome, twenty-five chapters; Ancient Geography; Natural Philosophy (Steele's).	Maintains a Medical College, also a College of Fine Arts, and a Post-Graduate course. Photography is taught in the College of Fine Arts, which also includes Architecture and Engraving.
To Quad., as above.	Plane, as above.		Common English, including Metric System, Physical Geography, and Natural Philosophy.	
Through Quad. (Loomis).	Plane, Loomis's four books.		Arithmetic, English Grammar, including Orthography, Modern Geography, Roman History in Worcester's Elements, Smith's Smaller History of Greece, Ancient Geography.	Students may pursue special courses of study. Scholarships provided for indigent students. Several prizes. Gymnasium, with exercise voluntary.
Olney's Introduction.	Pierce's Plane.		Common English, including Metric System, Smith's Roman History, outlines of Grecian History and Geography, a brief essay on some standard work in English literature, subjects announced in each annual catalogue.	Maintains a Theological course, also a course in Engineering. There are twenty-seven scholarships; also a goodly number of prizes.
Olney's Introduction.	Pierce's Plane.		Common English, including Metric System, Smith's Roman History, outlines of Grecian History and Geography, a brief essay on some standard work in English literature, subjects announced in each annual catalogue.	

NAME OF COLLEGE, OR UNIVERSITY.	Course.	LATIN.				GREEK, OR MODERN LANGUAGES.		
		Com. of Cæsar. No. of Books.	Virgil.	Orations of Cicero.	Latin Prose.	Books Anabasis.	Books Homer.	Greek Prose.
Union College (Non-sectarian), *Schenectady, New York.* Established 1795.	Classical.	Four. Also, Sal.'s Catil., or Jugurtha.[22]	Six of Æneid.	Six, including Milo.	Leighton's.	Three.	One.	Jones's.
	Scientific.							
Vanderbilt University (Southern Methodist), *Nashville, Tennessee.* Established 1873.	Classical.	Four, and Sal.'s Catiline.[27]	Four of Æneid.	Four Against Cat., also two books Livy.	Harkness, first part, or equivalent.	Two; also two of Memorabilia.		Jones's.
Vassar College, *Poughkeepsie, New York.* Woman's. Established 1861.	All courses.	Four.[27]	Six of Æneid, and six Eclogues.	Six.		Two.[28]		
Washington and Lee University (Non-sectarian), *Lexington, Virginia.* Established 1749.	Classical. (*See* GENERAL REMARKS.)	Four.[27]	Sallust instead of Virgil.	Ovid instead of Cicero.	Simple exercises.	Four.		Simple exercises.
Wellesley College (Non-sectarian), *Wellesley, Massachusetts.* Woman's. Established 1875.	All courses.	Four.[27]	Six of Æneid, and Eclogues.	Seven.	Harkness's Part I., or Arnold's twelve chapters, or Allen and Greenough's Part I.	Elective, until 1881. (*See* GENERAL REMARKS.)	Elective, until 1881.	Elective, until 1881.
	Scientific, in 1881.	Four.	Six of Æneid, Eclogues.	Seven.	Arnold's twelve chapters, or equivalent.	A thorough knowledge of French or German Grammar; ability to read at sight French or German prose, and to write a short composition. Students should prepare in both these languages.		

[27] Roman pronunciation.   [28] German or French will be accepted in place of Greek.

MATHEMATICS.				
Algebra.	Geometry.	Trigonometry.	MISCELLANEOUS.	GENERAL REMARKS.
To Quad.	Plane, five books.		Common English, including Metric System, and Ancient Geography.	Colleges of Medicine and Law, which are located at Albany. Maintains departments of Civil Engineering and Agriculture. Gymnasium exercise compulsory. Military tactics taught. There are a large number of scholarships, including prize scholarships; also medals and prizes.
To Quad.	Plane, five books.		Common English, including Metric System.	
Through Quad.	Plane.		Common English, including Metric System, Ancient Geography, and Mythology.	Maintains a Biblical, Law, and Medical Department; also Post-Graduate courses, and courses in Civil and Mining Engineering. Several medals, prizes, scholarships, and fellowships.
Through Quad. Olney's University.	Plane, Chauvenet, three books.		Common English, Guyot's Physical Geography, Ancient Geography, Hart's Rhetoric, Universal History (Weber's Outlines), first book.	Admits at sixteen. All students are required to take Latin, and to elect one of the following: Greek, German, or French. Maintains special courses, also a Preparatory Department for pupils at least fifteen years of age, who must be able to pass a satisfactory examination in common English.
To Quad.	Plane.		Common English.	The College does not designate its departments as Classical and Scientific, but is divided into Elective Schools, and students are allowed large liberty in choice of studies. Maintains a Law Department. Has a Gymnasium. Several prizes.
Olney's University to Part III.	First five books Loomis, or Olney's Plane.		Common English, including Metric System, Physical Geography, French or German.	Students must be sixteen on admission. In 1881, all candidates for Classical course must be fitted in Greek, Anabasis, four books; Iliad, three books; and simple exercises in prose composition, with same requirements in Latin as at present. Special opportunities are offered to teachers. There are courses for honors in Classics and Sciences; also, Post-Graduate courses. Has a large Gymnasium for the use of students. A prize of $250 will be given to the student who enters the Freshman Class in September, 1879 and 1880, best fitted in Latin, Greek, and Mathematics. To the one best fitted in Greek, $100; second, $75; third, $50; fourth, $25.
Olney's University, through Quad.	Olney's Plane.		Common English, including Metric System, Physical Geography.	

NAME OF COLLEGE, OR UNIVERSITY	Course.	LATIN. Com. of Cæsar, No. of Books.	Virgil.	Orations of Cicero.	Latin Prose.	GREEK, OR MODERN LANGUAGES. Books Anabasis.	Books Homer.	Greek Prose.
Wesleyan University (Methodist), *Middletown, Connecticut.* Both Sexes. Established 1831.	Classical.	??	Bucolics, Georgics, Six of Æneid.	Eight.	First two parts Harkness, or equivalent.	Four.	Three.	Simple exercises.
	Scientific.							
Williams College (Congregational), *Williamstown, Massachusetts.* Established 1793.	Classical. (all courses).	Four.[30]	Six of Æneid, and Georgics.	Seven.	Arnold's, to Passive Voice.	Four.	One.	
William and Mary's College (Non-sectarian, formerly Episcopalian), *Williamsburg, Virginia.* Established 1693.	Classical.	Four.[31]	Six of Æneid.			Four.		
	Scientific.							
Wisconsin State University (Non-sectarian), *Madison, Wisconsin.* Both Sexes. Established 1850.	Classical.	Four.[32]	Six of Æneid.	Eight.	First thirty-five chapters Allen's, comp., or equivalent.	Four.	Two.	Jones's.
	College of Arts.							
Yale College (Congregational), *New Haven, Connecticut.* Established 1701.	Classical.	Four.[29]	Six of Æneid, and Bucolics and Georgics.	Seven.	First twelve chapters Arnold.	Four.	Three.	Jones's or White's Lessons.
	Scientific.	Six.			First twelve chaps. Arnold, or Harkness's one hundred and twelve pages.			

[29] English pronunciation.   [30] English pronunciation used, Roman preferred.   [31] Roman pronunciation.

MATHEMATICS.			MISCELLANEOUS.	GENERAL REMARKS.
Algebra.	Geometry.	Trigonometry.		
Through Quad.	Five books Chauvenet, or equivalent.		Common English, including Metric System.	Students may pursue a Post-Graduate course. Long list of prizes. A Gymnasium is provided, with ample apparatus for exercise. Oldest Methodist College in the United States.
Loomis's to General Theory of Equations.	Chauvenet's, to Appendix I.	Chauvenet's, Part I., 8 chaps., large print, Part II., 2 chaps.	Common English, including Metric System.	
To Quad.	Two books Loomis (Books I. and III.).		English Grammar and Arithmetic, Geography, Ancient and Modern, Outlines Greek and Roman History.	Students may pursue a partial course. The income of over one hundred thousand dollars is devoted to scholarships for meritorious students. Long list of prizes.
To Quad.	Plane.		Common English.	Oldest college in the United States, except Harvard.
			Common English, especially Arithmetic.	
Elementary.	All Plane.		Common English, including Metric System, Physical Geography.	Maintains a Law School and Post-Graduate course; also, schools in Agriculture, Civil Engineering, Mechanical Engineering, Mining, Metallurgy; also, a school in Military Science. Military drill is required of Freshmen and Sophomores. Requirements for technical courses are same as for Sophomore Class of College of Arts.
Elementary.	All Plane.		Common English, including Metric System, Physical Geography, Physiology, Botany, Natural Philosophy.	
Loomis's to Logarithms.	Euclid two books, or Loomis's Books I., III., and IV.		English Grammar, Geography, and Arithmetic, including Metric System, Greek History (Smith's or Fyffe's).	Colleges of Law, Theology, Medicine, School of Fine Arts, Post-Graduate course. Several prizes. Scholarships and fellowships. Gymnasium for physical exercise; over one thousand students. Ladies admitted to School of Fine Arts.
Loomis's Treatise to General Theory of Equations.	Chauvenet nine books, or Loomis, with app. to Transversals.	Wheeler's or Richards's Plane.	English Grammar, U. S. History, Geography, and Arithmetic, including Metric System, Natural Philosophy—Snowball and Lund.	

This classification, in general, gives the number of pupils in attendance during the present college year of 1878–'79, although the statistics of a few colleges are from the Catalogues of one of the two previous years. It has been difficult in all cases to separate the students of the classical from those of the scientific and technical courses ; but, as these statistics are of special interest in view of the " new education " theory, great care has been taken to make them authentic, and in nearly all cases where the catalogues have failed to draw the lines of distinction the compiler has obtained the facts from direct correspondence

I. COLLEGES ADMITTING

NAME OF COLLEGE.	Students pursuing the Classical Course. [22]	Students pursuing Scientific and Technical Courses. [23]	Total in Academic Departments.	PROFESSIONAL	
				Medicine.	Law.
Columbia College.........	227	231	458	413	462
Harvard University.......	377	459	836	238	160
Yale College.............	587	166	753	58	68
Princeton College.........	377	39	416	No Med. Department.	No Law Department.
Dartmouth College........	212	69	281	160	No Law Department.
Union College............	88	80	168	123	92
Vanderbilt University....	52	74	126	171	26
Amherst College..........	317	10	327	No Med. Department.	No Law Department.
Lafayette College.........	161	99	260	No Med. Department.	No Report.
Brown University.........	195	20	215	No Med. Department.	No Law Department.
Bowdoin College..........	116	26	142	93	No Law Department.
Williams College.........	194	None.	194	No Med. Department.	No Law Department.
Hamilton College.........	160	None.	160	No Med. Department.	17
Rensselaer Polytechnic Institute.............	None.	166	166	No Med. Department.	No Law Department.
Rochester University.....	114	33	147	No Med. Department.	No Law Department.
Washington and Lee University.............	52	62	114	No Med. Department.	20
Trinity College...........	100	2	102	No Med. Department.	No Law Department.
Johns Hopkins University..	46	....	46	No Med. Department.	No Law Department.
Tufts College.............	55	19	74	No Med. Department.	No Law Department.
Kenyon College...........	32	8	40	No Med. Department.	No Law Department.
Middlebury College.......	56	None.	56	No Med. Department.	No Law Department.
Total...............	3,518	1,563	5,081	1,196	845

[22] Those who pursue both Latin and Greek.　　　　[23] Courses which do not require both Latin and Greek.

with the Presidents of the colleges, so that we believe them to be more nearly correct than those ever before published. The first list contains the Colleges which are at present open to gentlemen only, and have with one exception no preparatory department; the second list contains those which admit both sexes, and is classified according to sexes, and contains also the enumeration of students in the preparatory department. It will be noticed that, of the thirty-eight colleges, thirteen sustain preparatory schools, with a sum total of 1,652 gentlemen and 748 ladies.

GENTLEMEN ONLY.

SCHOOLS.	Other Schools.	Post-Graduates.	Grand Totals.	REMARKS.
Theology.				
No Theological Department,	No other Schools.	7	1,340	231 are in School of Mines. For college year of 1877–'78.
23	Agricultural School, 4; Dental School, 13.	52	1,326	Post-Graduates include candidates for higher degree; holders of fellowships and others not candidates for degrees. For college year of 1878–'79.
67	Fine Arts, 30; of whom 22 are ladies.	46	1,022	For college year of 1878–'79. Ladies admitted to School of Fine Arts.
No Theological Department.	Special Course, 11.	68	495	For college year of 1878–'79. Post-Graduates include 10 holders of fellowships.
No Theological Department.	Partial Course, 3.	1	385	For college year of 1878–'79.
No Theological Department.	No other Schools.	None.	383	Law and Medical Schools located at Albany.
59	No other Schools.	None.	382	Courses consist of a large number of schools in Elective studies. For college year of 1876–'77.
No Theological Department.	Partial Course, 6.	2	335	For college year of 1878–'79.
No Theological Department.	No other Schools.	7	267	For college year of 1877–'78.
No Theological Department.	Select Course, 14.	14	243	For college year of 1878–'79.
No Theological Department.	No other Schools.	None.	235	For college year of 1878–'79.
No Theological Department.	Partial Course, 14.	None.	208	For college year of 1878–'79.
No Theological Department.	No other Schools.	None.	177	For college year of 1878–'79.
No Theological Department.	No other Schools.	None.	166	Sustains only a course in Civil Engineering. For year of 1876–'77.
No Theological Department.	Eclectic Course, 6.	None.	153	For college year of 1877–'78.
No Theological Department.	No other Schools.	None.	134	For college year of 1876–'77.
No Theological Department.	Special Courses, 10.	None.	112	For college year of 1877–'78. Students in Special Courses must take Latin.
No Theological Department.	No other Schools.	58	104	No courses recognized. College largely Post-Graduate in its influence.
25	No other Schools.	None.	99	For college year of 1878–'79.
7	Preparatory School, 24; Irregulars, 3.	None.	74	For college year of 1877–'78.
No Theological Department.	No other Schools.	None.	56	For college year of 1878–'79.
181	138	253	7,696	

CLASSIFICATION OF UNIVERSITIES AND COLLEGES, IN REFERENCE TO THE NUMBER OF STUDENTS IN ATTENDANCE.

II. THOSE WHICH ADMIT BOTH SEXES.

NAME OF COLLEGE	STUDENTS PURSUING CLASSICAL COURSE, INCLUDING BOTH LATIN AND GREEK.			SCIENTIFIC AND TECHNICAL COURSES, NOT REQUIRING BOTH LATIN AND GREEK.			TOTAL IN ACADEMIC DEPARTMENT.			PROFESSIONAL SCHOOLS.								
										MEDICINE.			LAW.			THEOLOGY.		
	Gentlemen.	Ladies.	Total.	Gentlemen.	Ladies.	Total.	Gentlemen.	Ladies.	Total.	Gentlemen.	Ladies.	Total.	Gentlemen.	Ladies.	Total.	Gentlemen.	Ladies.	Total.
University of Michigan, Ann Arbor	162	33	195	191	39	230	353	72	425	Allopathy, 284 / Homœopathy, 48	41 / 12	325 / 60	465	2	465	No Theological Depart.		
Oberlin College, Oberlin, Ohio	126	35	161	16	139	155	144	172	316	No Medical Department.			No Law Department.			49	0	49
Northwestern University, Evanston, Illinois	73	6	79	65	47	112	138	53	191	153	0	153	124	1	125	106	0	108[33]
Boston University, Boston, Massachusetts	72	33	105	20[34]	0	20	92	33	125	122	62	184	142	0	143	105	3	108
University of Iowa, Iowa City	52	30	82	110	25	135	162	53	215	Allopathy, 74 / Homœopathy, 16	9 / 2	83 / 18	121	0	121	No Theological Depart.		
Chicago University, Chicago, Illinois	58	4	62	29	10	39	87	14	101	202	0	202	124	1	125	{ No Theological Department directly connected		
Cornell University, Ithaca, New York	53	7	60	355	46	401	408	53	461	No Medical Department.			No Law Department.			No Theological Depart.		
University of Wisconsin, Madison	58	4	62	96	44	140	154	48	202	No Medical Department.			48	0	48	No Theological Depart.		
Syracuse University, Syracuse, New York	71	4	75	36	13	49	107	17	124	43	5	48	No Law Department.			No Theological Depart.		

33 Distinct from the University, and called the "Garrett Biblical Institute."

34 College of Agriculture.

CLASSIFICATION OF UNIVERSITIES AND COLLEGES, IN REFERENCE TO THE NUMBER OF STUDENTS IN ATTENDANCE—(Continued).

II. THOSE WHICH ADMIT BOTH SEXES.

NAME OF COLLEGE.	OTHER SCHOOLS.			POST-GRADUATES.			PREPARATORY DEPARTMENT.			TOTALS, EXCLUDING PREPARATORY DEPARTMENT.			GRAND TOTALS, IN ALL DEPARTMENTS.			REMARKS.
	Gentlemen.	Ladies.	Total.	Gentlemen.	Ladies.	Total.	Gentlemen.	Ladies.	Total.	Gentlemen.	Ladies.	Total.	Gentlemen.	Ladies.	Total.	
University of Michigan, Ann Arbor.	Pharmacy, 69 | 0 | 69. Dental Surgery, 61 | 1 | 62. Music. 24 | 127 | 151			11	0	11	No Preparatory Dept.			1,229	128	1,357	1,229	128	1,357	For year 1878–'79.
Oberlin College, Oberlin, Ohio	Music.			1	0	1	340	158	498	218	299	517	558	457	1,016	For year 1878–'79.
Northwestern University, Evanston, Illinois	Music and Painting. 12 | 37 | 49			No Post-Graduates.			122	60	182	535	91	626	657	151	808	For year 1877–'78.
Boston University, Boston, Massachusetts	Music and Oratory. 46 | 57 | 103			14	1	15	No Preparatory Dept.			509	156	665	509	156	665	For year 1877–'78.
University of Iowa, Iowa City	Special Students. 2 | 4 | 6			9	0	9	133	67	200	377	68	445	510	135	645	(Academic Depart. of 1878–'79. Other Departm'ts of 1877–'78.
Chicago University, Chicago, Illinois	Elective Studies. 9 | 4 | 13			No Post-Graduates.			59	28	87	422	19	441	481	47	528	For year 1877–'78.
Cornell University, Ithaca, New York	No other Schools.			14	1	15	No Preparatory Dept.			422	54	476	422	54	476	For year 1878–'79.
University of Wisconsin, Madison	Special Students. 53 | 25 | 78			0	1	1	82	38	120	235	74	329	327	112	449	For year 1878–'79.
Syracuse University, Syracuse, New York	22	53	88 *	No Post-Graduates.			111	72	183 **	179	81	260	290	153	443	For year 1877–'78.

* Preparatory Schools not located at Syracuse.

** Mostly in College of Fine Arts.

CLASSIFICATION OF UNIVERSITIES AND COLLEGES, IN REFERENCE TO THE NUMBER OF STUDENTS IN ATTENDANCE.

II. THOSE WHICH ADMIT BOTH SEXES.

NAME OF COLLEGE	STUDENTS PURSUING CLASSICAL ORDER, INCLUDING BOTH LATIN AND GREEK.			SCIENTIFIC AND TECHNICAL COURSES, NOT REQUIRING BOTH LATIN AND GREEK.			TOTAL IN ACADEMIC DEPARTMENT.			PROFESSIONAL SCHOOLS.								
										MEDICINE.			LAW.			THEOLOGY.		
	Gentlemen.	Ladies.	Total.	Gentlemen.	Ladies.	Total.	Gentlemen.	Ladies.	Total.	Gentlemen.	Ladies.	Total.	Gentlemen.	Ladies.	Total.	Gentlemen.	Ladies.	Total.
Indiana Asbury, Greencastle........	142	13	185[22]	0	0	0	142	43	185	No Medical Department.			No Law Department.			10	0	10
University of California, Berkeley, California..................	57	6	63	211	46	257	268	52	320	31	4	35	$100,000 just presented for establishment of a Law Department.			No Theological Depart.		
Cornell College, Mount Vernon, Iowa.	17	4	21	40	22	62	57	26	83	No Medical Department.			No Law Department.			No Theological Depart.		
Illinois Industrial or State University, Urbana..................	82	34	116[39]	98	15	113	180	49	229	No Medical Department.			No Law Department.			No Theological Depart.		
University of Minnesota, Falls of St. Anthony....................	36	7	43	44	27	71	80	34	114	No Medical Department.			No Law Department.			No Theological Depart.		
Allegheny College, Meadville, Pennsylvania....................	43	6	49	35	4	39	69	10	79	No Medical Department.			No Law Department.			No Theological Depart.		
Wesleyan University, Middletown, Connecticut...................	127	3	130	23	2	25	150	5	155	No Medical Department.			No Law Department.			No Theological Depart.		
Simpson Centenary, Indianola, Iowa.	11	7	18	14	15	29	25	22	47	No Medical Department.			28	0	28	No Theological Depart.		
Colby University.................	114	10	124	0	0	0	114	10	124	No Medical Department.			No Law Department.			No Theological Depart.		
Totals...................	1,347	274	1,621	1,383	492	1,875	2,730	766	3,496	973	135	1,108	991	4*	995	272	3	275

22 Classical and Scientific.

39 Literature and Science.

CLASSIFICATION OF UNIVERSITIES AND COLLEGES, IN REFERENCE TO THE NUMBER OF STUDENTS IN ATTENDANCE—(Continued).

II. THOSE WHICH ADMIT BOTH SEXES.

NAME OF COLLEGE.	OTHER SCHOOLS.			POST-GRADUATES.			PREPARATORY DEPARTMENT.			TOTALS, EXCLUDING PREPARATORY DEPARTMENT.			GRAND TOTALS, IN ALL DEPARTMENTS.			REMARKS.
	Gentlemen.	Ladies.	Total.	Gentlemen.	Ladies.	Total.	Gentlemen.	Ladies.	Total.	Gentlemen.	Ladies.	Total.	Gentlemen.	Ladies.	Total.	
Indiana Asbury, Greencastle	13	5	18	No Post-Graduates.			138	69	218	165	48	213	323	108	431	For year 1877–'78.
University of California, Berkeley, California	College of Pharmacy. 33	4	37	4	0	4	No Preparatory Dept.			336	60	396	336	60	396	For year 1877–'78.
Cornell College, Mount Vernon, Iowa	Special Students. 1	1	2	No Post-Graduates.			188	117	305	58	27	85	246	144	390	For year 1877–'78.
Illinois Industrial or State University, Urbana	Music. 0	19	19	6	4	10	107	14	121	186	70	256	293	84	377	For year 1877–'78.
University of Minnesota, Falls of St. Anthony	Special Students. 44	26	70	No Post-Graduates.			111	76	187	124	60	184	235	136	371	For year 1877–'78.
Allegheny College, Meadville, Pennsylvania	Military Science. 139	0	139	No Post-Graduates.			175	51	226	79	10	89	254	41	295	For year 1877–'78.
Wesleyan University, Middletown, Connecticut	Special Students. 4	1	5	3	0	3	No Preparatory Dept.			157	6	163	157	6	163	For year 1878–'79.
Simpson Centenary, Indianola, Iowa	No other Schools.			No Post-Graduates.			42	27	69	53	22	75	95	49	144	For year 1877–'78.
Colby University	No other Schools.			No Post-Graduates.			No Preparatory Department directly connected.			114	10	124	114	10	124	For year 1877–'78.
Totals	556	365	991	55	7	62	1,628	748	2,376	5,418	1,283	6,701	7,046	2,031	9,077	

** Of whom 129 are otherwise mentioned.

†† Of which 171 are unclassified.

FACTS FROM THE ENUMERATION OF STUDENTS.

As a result of the increasing interest in the study of the sciences, and the desire on the part of colleges to have their courses suited to the individual taste and talent of students, many and important changes have been made in the courses of study. Some of the colleges, without encroaching upon the time-honored classics, have extended their curricula, thereby encouraging students to pursue post-graduate studies, as specialties; others have partially eliminated the Greek, to make room for the sciences; others still have substituted French or German for Greek in a so-called Latin-scientific course, and a few have abandoned distinct arbitrary courses entirely, and extended to students the privilege of electing their studies throughout the college curriculum.

To show how far these changes have affected the study of the classics—i. e., Latin and Greek—in different sections of the country, we present the following from the foregoing statistics:

In the thirteen colleges of the New England States, out of a total of 3,434 students in college departments, 2,568, or nearly seventy-five per cent., are in the classical course.

In the nine colleges of New York, New Jersey, and Pennsylvania, out of a total of 2,368 in college department, 1,302, or nearly fifty-four per cent., are in the classical course.

In the sixteen colleges west and south of Pennsylvania, out of a total of 2,941 in college department, 1,259, or less than forty-three per cent., are in the classical course.

These facts show that the students, in the colleges of the Western States particularly, are inclined to pursue the sciences and the modern languages, especially German, in the place of the Greek, while three fourths of all the students in the New England colleges still adhere to the study of the Greek.

In the colleges which admit both sexes, out of a total of 3,776 in the college department, 891, or nearly twenty-four per cent., are ladies. Of the 891 ladies in these colleges, 274, or nearly thirty-one per cent., are in the classical course; 492, or fifty-five per cent., are in the scientific or technical courses; 135 in the Medical Department; four in the Law Department; and three in the Theological Department; seven are in post-graduate courses, which is eleven per cent. of all in this department, and the remainder are pursuing studies in college departments, but not in regular courses. In the thirty-nine colleges, whose summary of students is given, there are more than 16,700 students, of whom 2,400 are in preparatory departments; 9,487 in the college department proper; 2,304 are pursuing the study of medicine; 1,840 the law; 456 theology; while 317 are in post-graduate courses. Of the entire number, 2,053 are ladies.

ANCIENT HISTORY AND CLASSICAL GEOGRAPHY.

THE college catalogues are largely indefinite in their statements of requirements for admission in these important branches, and, as a result, preparatory schools do not generally teach them with sufficient care and exactness, and students, on entering college, often find themselves sadly deficient in the systematic knowledge of the historical events and the geography of the classics which they have read.

All pupils in classics should provide themselves with a Classical Atlas (Appletons' or Long's) ; with a Classical Dictionary (Smith's or Anthon's) ; with a Dictionary of Antiquities (Anthon's) ; with Smith's History of Greece, Smith's, Merivale's, or Liddell's History of Rome, or equivalent books, and with Baird's Classical Manual. Let the study in these subjects be systematic and thorough, and students will find that the knowledge gained and the discipline secured, even though it may add a year to their preparatory work, will amply repay for the expense incurred and the time employed.

We therefore give on this page a more detailed account of the exact requirements of some of the universities, and earnestly recommend all students preparing for college to secure competent instruction in at least an average of what these several colleges require.

HARVARD UNIVERSITY

requires "Greek History to the death of Alexander; Roman History to the death of Commodus. Smith's smaller histories of Greece and Rome will serve to indicate the amount of knowledge demanded."

MICHIGAN UNIVERSITY

requires "In Grecian History the first three books of Smith's History of Greece, exclusive of the chapters on Literature and Art; an outline of Roman History from the foundation of the city to the battle of Actium." The university requires in Ancient Geography that particularly of Italy, Greece, and Asia Minor. Appletons' Hand-book or Atlas of Ancient Geography is undoubtedly the best; Long's Classical Atlas is also excellent.

CORNELL UNIVERSITY

requires "Smith's smaller history of Greece."

BOSTON UNIVERSITY

requires "History of Greece till its conquest by the Romans; History of Rome to Constantine. Smith's Manuals will suffice." Ancient Geography, "sufficient to illustrate all the authors read."

SYRACUSE UNIVERSITY

requires "Merivale's History of Rome, first twenty-five chapters; Smith's larger History of Greece, the first fourteen chapters. Ancient Geography, particularly that of Italy, Greece, and Asia Minor." Appletons' Hand-book or Atlas will suffice.

3

CLASSIFICATION OF COLLEGES AND UNIVERSITIES IN REFERENCE TO THE LATIN PRONUNCIATION IN USE OR PREFERRED

THE recent philological researches and discussions on the subject of Latin pronunciation have quite revolutionized the methods of pronunciation in the colleges and universities of our own country, and it becomes a matter of great interest and importance to the high schools and all college preparatory institutions which method prevails among the best classical scholars. It is not ours to judge, but we present below carefully-prepared statistics, tabulated from correspondence with the presidents or Latin professors in all these institutions. While it is true that no college refuses admission to a candidate who may be proficient in either the English, Roman, or so-called Continental pronunciation, it is nevertheless a lamentable fact that pupils applying for admission to colleges are rarely proficient in any particular method. The English and Roman methods are peculiarly distinct, and one or the other should be chosen and thoroughly taught. It will be noticed as a fact of interest that the two oldest colleges of New England differ in their preference : Harvard chooses the Roman, and Yale the English.

COLLEGES WHICH USE OR PREFER THE ENGLISH PRONUNCIATION.

NAME OF COLLEGE.	LOCATION.	LATIN PROFESSOR.
Amherst	Amherst, Mass.	Edward P. Crowell, A. M.
Bowdoin	Brunswick, Me.	John Avery, A. M.
Brown	Providence, R. I.	John L. Lincoln, LL. D.
Colby	Waterville, Me.	Julian D. Taylor, A. M.
Dartmouth	Hanover, N. H.	Rev. Henry Elijah Parker, A. M.
Hamilton	Clinton, N. Y.	Rev. Abel Grosvenor Hopkins, A. M.
Iowa State	Iowa City, Iowa	Amos N. Currier, A. M.
Kenyon	Gambier, Ohio.	Rev. Edward C. Benson, A. M.
Lafayette	Easton, Pa.	Rev. Lyman Coleman, D. D.
Northwestern	Evanston, Ill.	Daniel Bonbright, A. M.
Oberlin	Oberlin, Ohio	Giles W. Shurtleff, A. M.
Rochester [47]	Rochester, N. Y.	William C. Morey, A. M.
Simpson Centenary	Indianola, Iowa	C. H. Burke, M. A.
Syracuse	Syracuse, N. Y.	Frank Smalley, A. M.
Smith	Northampton, Mass.	Rev. Josiah Clark.
Trinity	Hartford, Conn.	George O. Holbrooke, M. A.
Tufts	College Hill, Mass.	Homan A. Dearborn, A. M.
Wesleyan	Middletown, Conn.	Rev. Calvin Sears Harrington, D. D.
Williams [48]	Williamstown, Mass.	Rev. Edward Herrick Griffin, A. M.
Yale	New Haven, Conn.	Thomas A. Thacher, LL. D.

[47] Continental also in use.   [48] English in use, but Roman preferred by Latin Department.

COLLEGES WHICH **USE OR** PREFER THE ROMAN PRONUNCIATION.

NAME OF COLLEGE.	LOCATION.	LATIN PROFESSOR.
Allegheny	Meadville, Pa	George W. Haskins, A. M.
Boston	Boston, Mass	Truman B. Kimpton, A. M.
California State	Oakland, Cal	Martin Kellogg, A. M.
Chicago	Chicago, Ill	Heman H. Sanford, A. M., Ph. D.
Columbia	New York City	Charles Short, LL. D.
Cornell	Mount Vernon, Iowa	Rev. Hugh Boyd, M. A.
Cornell	Ithaca, N. Y.	Tracy Peck, M. A.
Harvard	Cambridge, Mass	George Martin Lane, Ph. D.
Illinois Industrial	Urbana, Ill	James D. Crawford, M. A.
Indiana Asbury	Greencastle, Ind	Lewis L. Rogers, Ph. D.
Johns Hopkins	Baltimore, Md	Charles D. Morris, A. M.
Michigan State	Ann Arbor, Mich	Henry S. Frieze, LL. D.
Middlebury	Middlebury, Vt	Solon Albee, A. M.
Minnesota State	St. Anthony, Minn	Jabez Brooks, M. A., D. D.
Notre Dame **	Notre Dame, Ind	Rev. Thomas E. Walsh, C. S. C.
Princeton	Princeton, N. J.	William A. Packard, Ph. D.
Union	Schenectady, N. Y.	Rev. Robert T. S. Lowell, D. D.
Vanderbilt	Nashville, Tenn	B. W. Arnold, M. A.
Vassar	Poughkeepsie, N. Y.	Charles J. Hinkel, Ph. D.
Washington and Lee	Lexington, Va	Carter J. Harris, A. M.
Wellesley	Wellesley, Mass	Frances E. Lord.
William and Mary's	Williamsburg, Va	Rev. L. B. Wharton, A. M.
Williams **	Williamstown, Mass	Rev. Edward Herrick Griffin, A. M.
Wisconsin State	Madison, Wis	William F. Allen, A. M.

NOTE.—Excluding the two which seem to vibrate between the English, Roman, and Continental, or do not express a decided preference for either, we have twenty-two which use or prefer the Roman, eighteen the English, and one the Continental. All the Roman Catholic Institutions use the Continental.

** Continental.

ROMAN PRONUNCIATION.

HARVARD, Cornell (New York), and Michigan State Universities are, perhaps, the most prominent colleges which take the lead in earnestly recommending the adoption of this method, and we therefore give the scheme in detail as promulgated by these institutions, in their latest circulars.

These schemes are essentially the same, and do not materially differ from the method as found in the latest revised edition of Harkness's Latin Grammar, which also contains the fullest description of the English method, adhered to by many of the best universities in our country.

SCHEME OF MICHIGAN UNIVERSITY.

ROMAN PRONUNCIATION OF LATIN.—This university has adopted the following system of pronunciation, based upon the investigations of Corssen and other eminent philologists, and now employed in its essential features in the universities and leading schools of England and many institutions of this country, as being proved beyond question a close approximation to the Roman pronunciation in the time of Cicero.

VOWELS.

ā as in *father*, ă as in *amend*, or in *quaff* (not as in hat); ē as in *they*, ĕ as in *met*; ī as in *machine*, ĭ as in *pity*; ō as in *go*, ŏ as in *police* (not as in cot); ū as oo in *too*, ŭ as in *pull* (not as in but); y as i.

DIPHTHONGS.

In pronouncing the diphthongs the sound of both vowels is preserved.

ae as the word *ay*; au as ow in *power*; oe as oi in *oil*; eu nearly like u in *use*; u in *ua, ue,* etc., like w; ei as in *rein*.

CONSONANTS.

c always as in *can*; ch as k; g always as in *gun*; j always as y in *young*; s always as in *sin*; t always as in *tin*; v either as Fr. ou in *oui*, or like Eng. v.

SCHEME OF CORNELL UNIVERSITY.

To answer numerous inquiries in regard to the system of pronouncing Latin now adopted in this university, a statement of its essential deviations from the "English method" is herewith given. The system is, in no proper sense, "new": it is rather the result of investigations independently carried on in different countries and ages to ascertain how the Romans spoke their language at the period of its greatest purity.

VOWELS.

Each vowel had, in general, a single elementary sound. Though position somewhat modified the quality of this sound, yet the only important vocal distinction between "long" and "short" vowels was that of quantity. The following are approximate English equivalents of these vowel-sounds:

ā as in *father*, ă as in *dogma*; ē as in *they*, ĕ as in *valley*; ī as in *machine*, ĭ as in *unity*; ō as in *pole*, ŏ as in *police*; ū as in *rude*, ŭ as in *put*.

DIPHTHONGS.

In pronouncing the diphthongs, each element should have its own individual sound. But, as these two sounds are made with a single emission of breath, the practical analogies in English are these:

ae (or ai) as ai in *aisle*; au as ou in *house*; oe

(or oi) as *oi* in *oil*; *ei* as *ei* in *vein*; *eu* as *eu* in *feud*; *ui* as *ui* in *suite*.

SEMI-VOWEL.

j uniformly like *y*; *v* uniformly like *w*.

CONSONANTS.

c always like *k*; *g* always like *g* in *get*; *s* always like *s* in *sit*; *t* always like *t* in *till*.

SYLLABICATION.

A single consonant between vowels should be joined in pronunciation to the latter. Two or more consonants preceding a vowel should be uttered with that vowel, if the combined consonants begin a Latin (or Greek) word. In compound words, however, the component parts should be pronounced separately.

The above scheme is not claimed to be the exact Roman orthoëpy—the nature of the case must always preclude such absolute knowledge; it is, however, claimed to be so near an approach to the ancient pronunciation that there is full justification for the growing tendency to substitute its main features for the "English method" of speaking Latin—a method which came into being in quite modern times, which is so full of obvious defects that it satisfies few Latinists in England or America, and is an object of amazement and ridicule to classical scholars in other countries.

TRACY PECK,
Professor of Latin, Cornell University,
Ithaca, New York.

SCHEME OF HARVARD UNIVERSITY.

In Latin, the following pronunciation is recommended: *ä* as in *father*, *ă* the same sound, but shorter; *ē* like *ê* in *fête*, *ĕ* as in *set*; *ï* as in *machine*, *ĭ* as in *sit*; *ō* as in *hole*, *ŏ* as in *nor*; *ū* as in *rude*, *ŭ* as in *put*; *j* like *y* in *year*, *c* and *g* like Greek *κ* and *γ*.

NOTE.—In the so-called Continental method of pronunciation, the sounds of the vowels do not greatly differ from those of the Roman, but there is no fixed law for the sounds of the consonants, especially *c*, *g*, *j*, *v*; each continental nation yields to the analogies of its own language—for example, the French pronounce Cicero, *Seesayro*; the Germans, *Tseetsayro*; the Italians, *Cheechayro*; the Spaniards, *Theethayro*.

CLASSIFICATION OF COLLEGES AND UNIVERSITIES IN THE ORDER OF THEIR ESTABLISHMENT.

NAME OF COLLEGE OR UNIVERSITY.	LOCATION.	PRESIDENT.	Year established.
1. Harvard	Cambridge, Mass.	Charles W. Eliot, LL. D.	1638
2. William and Mary's	Williamsburg, Va.	Benjamin S. Ewell, LL. D.	1693
3. Yale	New Haven, Conn.	Rev. Noah Porter, D. D., LL. D.	1701
4. Princeton	Princeton, N. J.	Rev. James McCosh, D. D., LL. D.	1746
5. Washington and Lee	Lexington, Va.	Gen. G. W. C. Lee	1749
6. Columbia	City of New York.	Fred. A. P. Barnard, S. T. D., LL. D., L. H. D.	1754
7. Brown	Providence, R. I.	Rev. Ezekiel G. Robinson, D. D., LL. D.	1764
8. Dartmouth	Hanover, N. H.	Rev. Samuel C. Bartlett, D. D.	1769
9. Williams	Williamstown, Mass.	Paul A. Chadbourne, D. D., LL. D.	1793
10. Union	Schenectady, N. Y.	Rev. Eliphalet N. Porter, D. D.	1795
11. Middlebury	Middlebury, Vt.	Rev. Calvin B. Hulbert, D. D.	1797
12. Bowdoin	Brunswick, Me.	Joshua L. Chamberlain, LL. D.	1802
13. Hamilton	Clinton, N. Y.	Rev. Samuel G. Brown, D. D., LL. D.	1812
14. Allegheny	Meadville, Pa.	Rev. Lucius H. Bugbee, D. D.	1815
15. Colby	Waterville, Me.	Rev. Henry E. Robins, D. D.	1819
16. Amherst	Amherst, Mass.	Rev. Julius H. Seelye.	1821
17. Trinity	Hartford, Conn.	Rev. Thomas R. Pynchon, D.D., LL. D.	1823
18. Kenyon	Gambier, Ohio.	Rev. William B. Bodine, A. M.	1824
19. Rensselaer Polytechnic	Troy, N. Y.	Hon. James Forsyth.	1824
20. Wesleyan	Middletown, Conn.	Rev. Cyrus D. Foss, D. D.	1831
21. Lafayette	Easton, Pa.	Rev. William C. Cattell, D. D.	1832
22. Oberlin	Oberlin, Ohio.	Rev. J. H. Fairchild.	1833
23. Indiana Asbury	Greencastle, Ind.	Alexander Martin, D. D.	1837
24. Michigan	Ann Arbor, Mich.	James B. Angell, LL. D.	1841
25. Notre Dame	Notre Dame, Ind.	Very Rev. William Corby, C. S. C.	1842
26. Rochester	Rochester, N. Y.	Martin B. Anderson, LL. D.	1850
27. Wisconsin	Madison, Wis.	John Bascom, D. D., LL. D.	1850
28. Cornell	Mount Vernon, Iowa.	Rev. William F. King, D. D.	1851
29. California	Oakland, Cal.	John Le Conte, M. D.	1855
30. Northwestern	Evanston, Ill.	Oliver Marcy, LL. D. (Acting President)	1855
31. Tufts	College Hill, Mass.	Elmer H. Capen.	1855
32. Chicago	Chicago, Ill.	Rev. Galusha Anderson, D. D.	1859
33. Iowa State	Iowa City, Iowa.	Hon. Josiah L. Pickard, LL. D.	1860
34. Vassar	Poughkeepsie, N. Y.	Rev. Samuel L. Caldwell, D. D.	1861
35. Cornell	Ithaca, N. Y.	Hon. Andrew D. White, LL. D.	1865
36. Simpson Centenary	Indianola, Iowa.	Rev. T. C. Berry, A. M.	1866
37. Illinois Industrial	Urbana, Ill.	Rev. John M. Gregory, D. D., LL. D.	1868
38. Minnesota State	St. Anthony, Minn.	William T. Folwell	1868
39. Boston	Boston, Mass.	William F. Warren, S. T. D., LL. D.	1871
40. Syracuse	Syracuse, N. Y.	Rev. E. O. Haven, D. D., LL. D.	1872
41. Vanderbilt	Nashville, Tenn.	Landon C. Garland, LL. D.	1873
42. Wellesley	Wellesley, Mass.	Ada L. Howard.	1875
43. Smith	Northampton, Mass.	Rev. L. Clark Seelye, D. D., LL. D.	1875
44. Johns Hopkins Univers'y	Baltimore, Md.	Daniel C. Gilman, LL. D.	1876

CLASSIFICATION OF COLLEGES AND UNIVERSITIES IN REFERENCE TO THE ADMISSION OF THE SEXES.

Colleges exclusively for Gentlemen.

Amherst	Amherst, Mass.
Bowdoin	Brunswick, Me.
Brown	Providence, R. I.
Columbia	New York City.
Dartmouth	Hanover, N. H.
Hamilton	Clinton, N. Y.
Harvard [43]	Cambridge, Mass.
Johns Hopkins	Baltimore, Md.
Kenyon	Gambier, Ohio.
Lafayette	Easton, Pa.
Middlebury	Middlebury, Vt.
Notre Dame	Notre Dame, Ind.
Princeton	Princeton, N. J.
Rensselaer Polytechnic	Troy, N. Y.
Rochester	Rochester, N. Y.
Trinity	Hartford, Conn.
Tufts	College Hill, Mass.
Union	Schenectady, N. Y.
Vanderbilt	Nashville, Tenn.
Washington and Lee	Lexington, Va.
Williams	Williamstown, Mass.
William and Mary's	Williamsburg, Va.
Yale [44]	New Haven, Conn.

Colleges exclusively for Ladies.

Vassar	Poughkeepsie, N. Y.
Wellesley	Wellesley, Mass.
Smith	Northampton, Mass.

Colleges which admit Both Sexes.

Allegheny	Meadville, Pa.
Boston	Boston, Mass.
California State	Oakland, Cal.
Chicago	Chicago, Ill.
Colby	Waterville, Me.
Cornell (Iowa)	Mount Vernon, Iowa.
Cornell (New York)	Ithaca, N. Y.
Illinois Industrial	Urbana, Ill.
Indiana Asbury	Greencastle, Ind.
Iowa State	Iowa City, Iowa.
Michigan State	Ann Arbor, Mich.
Minnesota State	St. Anthony, Minn.
Northwestern	Evanston, Ill.
Oberlin	Oberlin, Ohio.
Simpson Centenary	Indianola, Iowa.
Syracuse	Syracuse, N. Y.
Wesleyan	Middletown, Conn.
Wisconsin State	Madison, Wis.

NOTE.—It is perhaps a significant fact that all the State universities, and all the colleges under the fostering care of the Methodist Church (so far as we have enumerated them), admit both sexes.

[43] *See* Harvard Examinations for Women, pages 48-50.   [44] Admits ladies to School of Fine Arts.

CLASSIFICATION OF COLLEGES AND UNIVERSITIES IN REFERENCE TO CHURCH INFLUENCE OR CONTROL.

VERY few of the colleges are sectarian in practice, but we classify them according to the church influence under which they were established, or by which they are generally fostered.

Methodist.

Boston University.
Cornell College (Iowa).
Indiana Asbury University.
Allegheny College.
Northwestern University.
Simpson Centenary College.
Syracuse University.
Wesleyan University.

Southern Methodist.

Vanderbilt University.

Congregational.

Amherst College.
Bowdoin College.
Dartmouth College.
Middlebury College.
Oberlin College.
Williams College.
Yale College.

Baptist.

Brown University.
Chicago University.
Colby University.
Rochester University.

Presbyterian.

Hamilton College.
Lafayette College.
Princeton College.

Episcopalian.

Columbia College.
Kenyon College.
Trinity College.

Universalist.

Tufts College.

Roman Catholic.

University of Notre Dame.

Non-Sectarian.

California State University.
Cornell University (New York).
Harvard University.
Illinois Industrial University.
Iowa State University.
Johns Hopkins University.
Michigan State University.
Minnesota State University.
Rensselaer Polytechnic Institute.
Smith College.
Union College.
Vassar College.
Washington and Lee University.
Wellesley College.
William and Mary's College.[47]
Wisconsin State University.

[47] Formerly Episcopalian.

REQUIREMENTS FOR ADMISSION TO THE UNIVERSITIES AND COLLEGES IN THE UNITED STATES.

The forty-four colleges whose specific requirements for admission have been given, fairly represent all the universities and colleges of the country. We give below an average of these requirements, a thorough preparation in which will, we believe, admit a student to any of the institutions whose specific requirements are not stated.

I. CLASSICAL COURSE.

LATIN.

Four books of Cæsar (Harkness's edition recommended) ; six books of Virgil's Æneid (Frieze's or Bryce's recommended) ; eight orations of Cicero, including the Manilian Law (Harkness's recommended) ; the first two parts of Harkness's Latin Prose Composition, or forty-four exercises in Arnold's or an equivalent, with a thorough knowledge of the Latin Grammar, including Prosody (Harkness's recommended).

GREEK.

Xenophon's Anabasis, three books (Boise's recommended) ; two books of Homer's Iliad (Boise's recommended), omitting Catalogue of Ships, Book II. ; simple exercises in Greek Prose Composition, with accents, as may be found in the first lessons of Arnold's, Boise's, or Jones's Greek Prose, with a thorough knowledge of the Greek Grammar (Hadley's or Goodwin's recommended).

MATHEMATICS.

Arithmetic, including Metric System ; Algebra to Quadratics (Loomis's or Olney's recommended) ; Plane Geometry (Loomis, Olney, Wentworth, or Chauvenet).

ANCIENT HISTORY AND CLASSICAL GEOGRAPHY.

History as found in Smith's smaller histories of Greece and Rome. Classical Geography should be studied from such a book as Appletons' Hand-book, or Long's.

COMMON ENGLISH.

A thorough knowledge of English Grammar, with such proficiency in the elements of Rhetoric as will enable the student to spell, punctuate, and paragraph correctly ; United States History, Political and Mathematical Geography, with elements of Physical Geography.

II. SCIENTIFIC COURSE.

To enter the Scientific courses, a student should have an elementary knowledge of Natural Philosophy, or Botany, or Chemistry ; the Science Primers will indicate the amount. The same proficiency in Mathematics as mentioned above, with Algebra *through* Quadratics, and French and German instead of Latin and Greek, or Latin, with French or German, instead of Greek.

ABBREVIATIONS USED.

M. E.	Methodist Episcopal.	S. P.	Southern Presbyterian.	C. and P.	Congregational and Presbyterian.
M. E. S.	Methodist Episcopal South.	Cong.	Congregationalist.	Mor.	Moravian.
M. P.	Methodist Protestant.	P. E.	Protestant Episcopal.	N. C.	New Church.
A. M. E.	African Methodist Episcopal.	Luth.	Lutheran.	Jew.	Jewish.
Bap.	Baptist.	Chr.	Christian.	E. A.	Evangelical Association.
F. B.	Free Baptist.	Univ.	Universalist.	Mas.	Masonic.
F. W. B.	Free-Will Baptist.	U. B.	United Brethren.	State.	State Universities.
S. D. B.	Seventh-Day Baptist.	Unit.	Unitarian.	Non-Sec.	Non-Sectarian.
Pres.	Presbyterian.	R. C.	Roman Catholic.	U. S. G.	United States Government.
U. P.	United Presbyterian.	Fr.	Friends.	——	Unknown.
C. P.	Cumberland Presbyterian.	G. R.	German Reformed.	*	Admits both sexes.
A. R. P.	Associated Reformed Presbyterian.	Ref.	Reformed (Dutch).	†	Exclusively for ladies.

STATE.	Location.	Church or other Control.	STATE.	Location.	Church or other Control.
Maine.			**New York** (continued).		
Bates College *	Lewiston	F. B.	St. Lawrence University *	Canton	Univ.
BOWDOIN COLLEGE	Brunswick	Cong.	St. Stephen's College	Annandale	P. E.
COLBY UNIVERSITY *	Waterville	Bap.	SYRACUSE UNIVERSITY *	Syracuse	M. E.
New Hampshire.			UNION COLLEGE	Schenectady	Non-Sec.
DARTMOUTH COLLEGE	Hanover	Cong.	University of City of New York *	New York City	Non-Sec.
Vermont.			UNIVERSITY OF ROCHESTER	Rochester	Bap.
MIDDLEBURY COLLEGE	Middlebury	Cong.	VASSAR COLLEGE †	Poughkeepsie	Non-Sec.
Norwich University	Northfield	P. E.	Wells College †	Aurora	Non-Sec.
University of Vermont *	Burlington	Non-Sec.	Martin Luther College	Buffalo	Luth.
Massachusetts.			**New Jersey.**		
AMHERST COLLEGE	Amherst	Cong.	COLLEGE OF NEW JERSEY.	Princeton	Pres.
Boston College	Boston	R. C.	Rutgers College	New Brunswick	Ref.
BOSTON UNIVERSITY *	Boston	M. E.	St. Benedict's College	Newark	R. C.
College of the Holy Cross	Worcester	R. C.	Seton Hall College	South Orange	R. C.
HARVARD COLLEGE	Cambridge	Non-Sec.	Burlington College	Burlington	P. E.
SMITH COLLEGE †	Northampton	Non-Sec.	**Pennsylvania.**		
TUFTS COLLEGE	College Hill	Univ.	ALLEGHENY COLLEGE *	Meadville	M. E.
WELLESLEY COLLEGE †	Wellesley	Non-Sec.	Dickinson College	Carlisle	M. E.
WILLIAMS COLLEGE	Williamstown	Cong.	Franklin and Marshall College	Lancaster	G. R.
Rhode Island.			Haverford College	West Haverford	Fr.
BROWN UNIVERSITY	Providence	Bap.	LAFAYETTE COLLEGE.	Easton	Pres.
Connecticut.			La Salle College	Philadelphia	R. C.
TRINITY COLLEGE	Hartford	P. E.	Lebanon Valley College *	Annville	U. B.
WESLEYAN UNIVERSITY *	Middletown	M. E.	Lehigh University	South Bethlehem	P. E.
YALE COLLEGE	New Haven	Cong.	Lincoln University	Oxford	Pres.
New York.			Mercersburg College	Mercersburg	G. R.
Alfred University *	Alfred	S. D. B.	Monongahela College *	Jefferson	Bap.
Canisius College	Buffalo	R. C.	Moravian College	Bethlehem	Mor.
Col. of City of New York	New York City	City.	Muhlenberg College	Allentown	Luth.
Col. of St. Francis Xavier	New York City	R. C.	Newcastle College *	Newcastle	Non-Sec.
COLUMBIA COLLEGE	New York City	P. E.	Palatinate College *	Myerstown	G. R.
CORNELL UNIVERSITY *	Ithaca	Non-Sec.	Pennsylvania College †	Gettysburg	Luth.
Elmira Female College †	Elmira	Pres.	St. Francis College	Loretto	R. C.
HAMILTON COLLEGE	Clinton	Pres.	St. Joseph's College	Philadelphia	R. C.
Hobart College	Geneva	P. E.	St. Vincent's College	Batty's	R. C.
Ingham University †	Le Roy	Pres.	Swarthmore College *	Swarthmore	Fr.
Madison University	Hamilton	Bap.	Thiel College *	Greenville	Luth.
Manhattan College	New York City	Non-Sec.	University of Lewisburg	Lewisburg	Bap.
Rutgers Female College †	New York City	Non-Sec.	Univer. of Pennsylvania	Philadelphia	State.
RENSSELAER POLYTECHNIC INSTITUTE	Troy	Non-Sec.	Ursinus College	Freeland	Ref.
St. Bonaventure's College	Allegany	R. C.	Villanova College	Villanova	R. C.
St. Francis College	Brooklyn	R. C.	Wash. and Jefferson Col.	Washington	Pres.
St. John's College	Brooklyn	R. C.	Waynesburg College *	Waynesburg	C. P.
St. Joseph's College	Fordham, N. Y. C.	R. C.	Western Univer. of Pa.	Pittsburg	Non-Sec.
St. John's College	Buffalo	R. C.	Westminster College *	New Wilmington	U. P.

STATE.	Location.	Church or other Control.	STATE.	Location.	Church or other Control.
Delaware.			**Mississippi** (continued).		
Delaware College	Newark	State.	Shaw University *	Holly Springs	M. E.
Maryland.			Alcorn University *	Rodney	Non-Sec.
Frederick College	Frederick	State.	Oakland College	Oakland	Pres.
Johns Hopkins Univer.	Baltimore	Non-Sec.	University of Mississippi	Oxford	State.
Loyola College	Baltimore	R. C.	Pass Christian College	Pass Christian	R. C.
Rock Hill College	Ellicott City	R. C.	Madison College	Sharon	
St. Charles College	Ellicott City	R. C.	Tongaloo University	Tongaloo	
St. John's College	Annapolis	State.	Jefferson College	Washington	
Washington College	Chestertown	Non-Sec.	**Louisiana.**		
Wes. Maryland College *	Westminster	M. P.	Thomson University	Baldwin	M. E.
Mount St. Mary's	Emmetsburg	R. C.	Louisiana State	Baton Rouge	State.
Mount St. Clement's	Ilchester	R. C.	St. Charles College	Grand Coteau	R. C.
Calvert College	New Windsor	R. C.	Mount Lebanon Univer.	Mount Lebanon	Bap.
Virginia.			Centenary College	Jackson	M. E. S.
College of William and Mary	Williamsburg	Non-Sec.	College of the Immaculate Conception	New Orleans	R. C.
Emory and Henry Col.	Emory	M. E. S.	Leland University *	New Orleans	Bap.
Hampden-Sidney College	Hampden-Sidney	Pres.	Straight University *	New Orleans	Cong.
Randolph-Macon College	Ashland	M. E. S.	Jefferson College	St. James	R. C.
Richmond College	Richmond	Bap.	New Orleans University *	New Orleans	M. E.
Roanoke College	Salem	Luth.	**Texas.**		
University of Virginia	Univer. of Va. P. O.	State.	St. Joseph's College	Brownville	R. C.
Wash. and Lee Univer.	Lexington	Non-Sec.	Colorado College	Columbia	Luth.
West Virginia.			University of St. Mary	Galveston	R. C.
Bethany College	Bethany	Chr.	Henderson College *	Henderson	Non-Sec.
West Virginia College	Flemington	F. W. B.	Baylor University	Independence	Bap.
West Virginia University	Morgantown	State.	St. Mary's College	San Antonio	R. C.
St. Vincent's College	Wheeling	R. C.	Waco University *	Waco	Bap.
North Carolina.			Wiley University *	Marshall	M. E.
Biddle University	Charlotte	Pres.	Guadelupe College	Seguin	R. C.
Davidson College	Davidson Col. P. O.	Pres.	Salado College *	Salado	Non-Sec.
North Carolina College	Mount Pleasant	Luth.	Southwestern University	Georgetown	M. E. S.
Rutherford College *	Happy Home	M. E.	Trinity University *	Tehuacana	C. P.
Trinity College	Trinity	M. E. S.	**Arkansas.**		
Univer. of North Carolina	Chapel Hill	State.	Arkansas College *	Batesville	Pres.
Wake Forest College	Forestville	Bap.	Cane Hill College *	Boonsboro	C. P.
Weaverville College *	Weaverville	Non-Sec.	Ark. Industrial Univer.	Fayetteville	Non-Sec.
Wilson College *	Wilson	Non-Sec.	Judson University *	Judsonia	Bap.
Yadkin College	Yadkin Col. P. O.	Non-Sec.	St. John's College	Little Rock	Mas.
South Carolina.			**Kentucky.**		
College of Charleston	Charleston	Non-Sec.	Berea College *	Berea	Cong.
Erskine College	Due West	A. R. P.	Bethel College	Russellville	Bap.
Furman University	Greenville	Bap.	Cecilian College	Cecilian	R. C.
Newberry College	Walhalla	Luth.	Central University	Richmond	S. P.
Nofford College	Spartanburgh	M. E. S.	Centre College	Danville	Pres.
Univer. of South Carolina	Columbia	State.	Concord College *	New Liberty	Bap.
Georgia.			Eminence College *	Eminence	Chr.
Atlanta University *	Atlanta	Non-Sec.	Georgetown College	Georgetown	Bap.
Clark University *	Atlanta	M. E.	Ghent College *	Ghent	Non-Sec.
Emory College	Oxford	M. E. S.	Kentucky University	Lexington	State.
Gainesville College *	Gainesville	Non-Sec.	Kentucky Wesley. Univ.	Millersburg	M. E. S.
Mercer University	Macon	Bap.	St. Joseph's College	Bardstown	R. C.
Pio Nono College	Macon	R. C.	St. Mary's College	St. Mary's	R. C.
University of Georgia	Athens	State.	Warren College	Bowling Green	M. E. S.
Oglethorpe College	Atlanta	Pres.	**Missouri.**		
Christ's College	Montpelier	P. E.	University of Missouri *	Columbia	State.
Alabama.			Baptist College *	Louisiana	Bap.
Southern University	Greensboro	M. E. S.	Central College	Fayette	M. E. S.
Howard College	Marion	Bap.	St. Vincent's College	Cape Girardeau	R. C.
Spring Hill College	Mobile	R. C.	Westminster College	Fulton	S. P.
University of Alabama	Tuscaloosa	State.	Lewis College *	Glasgow	M. E.
East Alabama College	Auburn	M. E. S.	Jefferson City College	Jefferson City	P. E.
Talladega College	Talladega		William Jewell College	Liberty	Bap.
Mississippi.			Palmyra College	Palmyra	P. E.
Simple-Braddus College	Centre Hill	Bap.	St. Charles College	St. Charles	M. E. S.
Mississippi College	Clinton	Bap.	Central Wesleyan Col. *	Warrenton	M. E.
			Christian Brothers Col.	St. Louis	R. C.

STATE.	Location.	Church or other Control.	STATE.	Location.	Church or other Control.
Missouri (continued).			**Ohio** (continued).		
Christian University *...	Canton	Chr.	Muskingien College	New Concord....	Non-Sec.
Drury College........	Springfield.....	Cong.	Miami University*.....	Springboro.....	Fr.
Grand River College..	Edinburg....	Bap.	Wittenberg College*....	Springfield.....	Luth.
La Grange College *....	La Grange	Bap.	Heidelberg College*....	Tiffin.....	Ref.
Lincoln College.......	Greenwood	U. P.	Urbana University.....	Urbana.....	N. C.
St. Louis University....	St. Louis....	R. C.	Otterbein University* ..	Westerville.....	U. B.
Thayer College *......	Kidder....	Cong.	Willoughby College*	Willoughby	M. E.
Washington University..	St. Louis.....	Non-Sec.	University of Wooster*	Wooster.....	Pres.
Hannibal College..	Hannibal,......	—	Antioch College*	Yellow Springs,.....	Unit.
Johnson College.. ...	Macon City.....	—	Wilberforce University*.	Xenia.....	A. M. E.
St. Joseph's College. ...	St. Joseph.....	R. C.	Xenia College*..	Xenia.....	M. E.
Tennessee.			Ohio Wes. University*	Delaware.....	M. E.
University of Nashville..	Nashville.......	State.	One-Study University*.	Scio Post-Office..	M. E.
East Ten. Wes. Univer.*	Athens	M. E.	**Ohio Central College***	Iberia.....	U. P.
King College.......	Bristol.......	Pres.	**Hiram College***...	Hiram.....	Chr.
Greenville and Tusculum College * ...	Tusculum.....	Pres.	**OBERLIN COLLEGE***	Oberlin.....	Cong.
Bethel College *...	McKenzie.....	C. P.	**Geneva College*.** ..	West Geneva.....	Pres.
Central Tennessee Col.*.	Nashville.....	M. E.	**Hebrew Union College*.**	Cincinnati.....	Jew.
Christian Brothers Col..	Memphis......	R. C.	**KENYON COLLEGE.**	Gambler.....	P. E.
Cumberland University *	Lebanon.....	C. P.	McCorcle College*	Sago.....	Pres.
East Tennessee Univer..	Knoxville.....	Non-Sec.	University of Cincinnati*	Cincinnati.....	Non-Sec.
Fisk **University** * ...	Nashville.....	Non-Sec.	Wilmington College* ..	Wilmington.....	Fr.
Henderson **Masonic** *..	Henderson	Non-Sec.	**Indiana.**		
Hiwassee College	**Hiwassee Col. P.O.**	M. E. S.	**Indiana University*...**	Bloomington.....	State.
McKenzie College *....	McKenzie.....	Non-Sec.	**Brookville College***	Brookville.....	M. E.
Manchester College*...	Manchester.....	Non-Sec.	**Wabash College**	Crawfordsville.....	Pres.
Maryville College*...	Maryville.....	Pres.	**Franklin College*......**	Franklin.....	Bap.
Mosheim College*....	Mosheim.....	Luth.	**Fort Wayne College*...**	Fort Wayne.....	M. E.
Mossy Creek College ...	Mossy Creek...	Bap.	**Concordia College.....**	Fort Wayne.....	Luth.
Neophogen College*....	Gallatin.....	Non-Sec.	Hanover **College.....**	Hanover.....	Pres.
So. Wes. Bap. Univ....	Jackson.....	Bap.	Hartsville **University....**	Hartsville.....	U. B.
So. Wes. Pres. **Univ.** ...	Clarksville.....	Pres.	**North** Wes. **Chr. Univ.**	Indianapolis.....	Chr.
Univ. of South........	Sewanee.....	P. E.	Union Christian College*	Merom.....	Chr.
VANDERBILT UNIVERSITY.	Nashville.....	M. E. S.	Moores Hill College* ..	Moore's Hill.....	M. E.
Woodbury College*....	Woodbury.....	Non-Sec.	Purdue University	Lafayette.....	Non-Sec.
Pres. Synodical College.	La Grange.....	Pres.	Salem College.....	Bourbon.....	Bap.
Jonesborough College ..	Jonesborough.....	M. E.	UNIV. OF NOTRE-DAME.	Notre Dame.....	R. C.
Union University......	Murfreesboro,.....	Bap.	Earlham College*.....	Richmond.....	Fr.
Franklin College.......	Near Nashville...	Chr.	St. Meinrad's College..	St. Meinrad's.....	R. C.
Michigan.			Valparaiso College.....	Valparaiso.....	
Adrian College*........	Adrian,........	M. P.	Smithson College*	Logansport.....	Univ.
Albion College*........	Albion........	M. E.	Howard College.....	Kokomo.....	
St. Philip's College....	Detroit.....	R. C.	Ridgeville College*.....	Ridgeville.....	F. W. B.
Hillsdale College*.......	Hillsdale.....	F. W. B.	INDIANA ASBURY UNIV.*.	Greencastle.....	M. E.
Hope College*........	Holland	Ref.	Butler University*.....	Irvington.....	Chr.
Kalamazoo College*...	Kalamazoo.....	Bap.	Bedford College*......	Bedford.....	Chr.
Olivet College*........	Olivet.....	Cong.	**Illinois.**		
UNIVERSITY OF MICHIGAN.............	Ann Arbor......	State.	ILL. INDUSTRIAL UNIV.*	Urbana.....	State.
Grand Traverse*. ...:	Benzonia.......	Cong.	Abingdon College*.....	Abingdon.....	Chr.
Battle Creek College* ..	Battle Creek.....	S. D. B.	Illinois Wes. Univ.*....	Bloomington.....	M. E.
Ohio.			St. Viateur's College...	Kankakee.....	R. C.
Ohio University*.......	Athens. ..	State.	Blackburn University*..	Carlinville.....	Pres.
Buchtel College*......	Athens... ..	Univ	St. Ignatius College.....	Chicago.....	R. C.
Baldwin University*....	Berea ..	M. E.	St. Aloysius College....	East St. Louis ...	R. C.
German Wallace Col.*..	Berea ..	M. E.	Eureka College*.....	Eureka.....	Chr.
St. Xavier's College	Cincinnati ..	R. C.	Lombard University*...	Galesburg.....	Univ.
Mount St. Mary's of the West........	Cincinnati,.....	R. C.	Knox College*......	Galesburg.....	Cong.
Farmer's College......	College Hill	Non-Sec.	Illinois College*......	Jacksonville.....	Cong.
Capitol University......	Columbus.....	Luth.	McKendree College*...	Lebanon.....	M. E.
Denison University.....	Granville.....	Bap.	Lincoln University*.....	Lincoln.....	C. P.
Harlem Springs College.	Harlem Springs..		Monmouth College*	Monmouth.....	U. P.
Western Reserve College	Hudson......	Non-Sec.	Northwestern College* ..	Naperville.....	E. A.
St. Louis College.... ..	Louisville.......	R. C	Augustina College.....	Rock Island.....	Luth.
Marietta College......	Marietta.....	C. & P	Quincy College*.....	Quincy.....	M. E.
Mount Union*........	Mount Union.....	M. E.	Jubilee College.....	Robin's Nest...	P. E.
Franklin College.......	New Athens....	U. P	Shurtleff College*.....	Upper Alton....	Bap.
			Westfield College*.....	Westfield.....	U. B.
			Wheaton College*.....	Wheaton.....	Cong.
			UNIV. OF CHICAGO*.....	Chicago.....	Bap.

STATE.	Location.	Church or other Control.	STATE.	Location.	Church or other Control.
Illinois (*continued*).			**Kansas** (*continued*).		
St. Joseph's College....	Lentopolis.......	R. C.	Washburn College*....	Topeka.........	Cong.
Rock River University*.	Dixon	Non-Sec.	Lane University.......	Lecompton......	U. B.
NORTHWESTERN UNIV.*..	Evanston........	M. E.	St. Mary's College.....	St. Mary......	R. C.
Lake Forest University*.	Lake Forest.....	Pres.	**Nebraska.**		
Ill. Agri. College*......	Irvington.......	Non-Sec.	University of Nebraska*	Lincoln........	State.
Hedding College*.....	Abingdon.......	M. E.	Doane College*.......	Crete.........	Cong.
Ewing College*.......	Ewing..........	Non-Sec.	Nebraska College.....	Nebraska City...	P. E.
Carthage College*.....	Carthage.......	Luth.	Congregational College..	Fontenelle......	Cong.
Wisconsin.			**Oregon.**		
UNIV. OF WISCONSIN*...	Madison.......	State.	University of Oregon*..	Eugene City....	State.
Laurence University*...	Appleton.......	M. E.	Christian College*.....	Monmouth......	Chr.
Wayland University....	Beaver Dam.....	Bap.	Corvallis College*....	Corvallis......	M. E. S.
Beloit College.........	Beloit.........	Cong.	McMinnville College*...	McMinnville....	Bap.
Galesville University*..	Galesville......	M. E.	Pacific University*.....	Forest Grove...	E. A.
Janesville College......	Janesville......	----	Philomath College*.....	Philomath......	U. B.
Pio Nono College	St. Frances....	R. C.	Willamette University*..	Salem.........	M. E.
Milton College*........	Milton.........	S. D. B.	Holy Angels' College...	Vancouver.....	R. C.
Racine College	Racine........	P. E.	Oregon College.......	Oregon City....	Bap.
Ripon College*.......	Ripon.........	Cong.	**Colorado.**		
St. John's College.....	Prairie du Chien.	R. C.	University of Colorado..	Boulder.......	State.
Northwestern Univ.*...	Watertown.....	Luth.	**California.**		
Carroll College	Waukesha......	Pres.	UNIVERSITY OF CALIFOR-		
Minnesota.			NIA*.............	Berkeley....	State.
UNIV. OF MINNESOTA*...	Falls of St. Ant'ny.	State.	College of St. Augustine.	Benicia......	P. E.
St. John's College.....	St. Joseph......	R. C.	St. Vincent's College....	Los Angeles....	R. C.
Carleton College*.....	Northfield......	Cong.	Marysville College.....	Marysville......	
Iowa.			Petaluma College	Petaluma......	Bap.
IOWA STATE UNIV.*	Iowa City......	State.	St. Ignatius College	San Francisco...	R. C.
Burlington University *.	Burlington......	Bap.	St. Mary's College.....	San Francisco...	R. C.
Griswold College	Davenport......	P. E.	University College.....	San Francisco...	----
Nor. Lutheran College..	Decorah.......	Luth.	San Rafael College.....	San Rafael.....	R. C.
Fairfield College*.....	Fairfield......	Luth.	Franciscan College.....	Santa Barbara...	R. C.
Upper Iowa University*.	Fayette	M. E.	College of Our Lady of		
Iowa College*........	Grinnell.......	Cong.	Guadelupe........	Santa Inez.....	R. C.
Iowa Wesleyan Univ.*..	Mount Pleasant..	M. E.	Univ. of the Pacific*...	Santa Clara....	M. E.
Central Univ. of Iowa*.	Pella..........	Bap.	Pacific Methodist Col.*.	Santa Rosa....	M. E. S.
Humboldt College*.....	Springfield.....	Unit.	Pacific Methodist Col.* .	Vacaville.......	M. E.
Tabor College*........	Tabor.........	Cong.	California College*.....	Vacaville.......	Bap.
CORNELL COLLEGE*.....	Mount Vernon...	M. E.	Hesperian College*.....	Woodland......	Chr.
German College*.......	Mount Pleasant..	M. E.	Pierce Christian Col.*...	College City....	Chr.
Oskaloosa College*.....	Oskaloosa......	Chr.	Sacred Heart College...	San Francisco...	R. C.
Parson's College*.....	Fairfield	Pres.	Santa Clara College	Santa Clara....	R. C.
Penn College*........	Oskaloosa......	Fr.	Washington College*....	Washington....	Non-Sec.
SIMPSON CENTENARY COL.*	Indianola......	M. E.	**District of Columbia.**		
Univ. of Des Moines*...	Des Moines....	Bap.	Georgetown College	Georgetown....	R. C.
Western College*......	Western.......	U. B.	Columbian College	Washington.....	Bap.
Algona College*.......	Algona........	M. E.	Gonzaga College.......	Washington.....	R. C.
Amity College*.......	College Spring..	Non-Sec.	Howard University*....	Washington.....	Cong.
Kansas.			Nat. Deaf Mute College..	Washington.....	Non-Sec.
State University*......	Lawrence.......	State.	**United States Govern-**		
St. Benedict's College...	Atchison.......	R. C.	**ment.**		
Baker University*.....	Baldwin City ...	M. E.	U. S. Naval Academy...	Annapolis, Md...	U. S. G.
Highland University*...	Highland.......	Pres.	U. S. Military Academy.	West Point, N. Y.	U. S. G.
Ottawa University*.....	Ottawa........	Bap.			

NOTE.—Excluding the Roman Catholic Institutions, none of which admit ladies, there are **three hundred and fifty-five universities** and colleges, of which one hundred and eighty-three, or fifty-two per cent., admit both sexes.

CLASSIFICATION OF UNIVERSITIES AND COLLEGES BY STATES,

Giving the Ratio in each State to Population.

NAMES OF STATES.	POPULATION.[*]	NUMBER OF COLLEGES.	RATIO OF COLLEGES TO POPULATION.
Maine	626,915	3	1 to 208,972
New Hampshire	318,300	1	1 " 318,300
Vermont	330,551	3	1 " 110,184
Massachusetts	1,457,351	9	1 " 161,928
Rhode Island	217,353	1	1 " 217,353
Connecticut	537,454	3	1 " 179,151
Total in New England States	3,487,924	20	1 to 174,396
New York	4,382,759	28	1 to 156,527
New Jersey	906,096	5	1 " 181,219
Pennsylvania	3,521,951	29	1 " 121,447
Delaware	125,015	1	1 " 125,015
Maryland	780,894	11	1 " 70,990
Virginia	1,225,163	8	1 " 153,145
West Virginia	442,014	4	1 " 110,503
District of Columbia	131,700	5	1 " 26,340
Total in Middle States, including District of Columbia	11,515,592	91	1 to 126,545
North Carolina	1,071,361	10	1 to 107,136
South Carolina	705,606	6	1 " 117,601
Georgia	1,184,109	9	1 " 131,568
Alabama	996,992	6	1 " 166,165
Florida	187,748	0	....
Tennessee	1,258,520	27	1 to 46,612
Total in Southeastern States	5,404,336	58	1 to 93,178
Kentucky	1,321,011	14	1 to 94,358
Ohio	2,665,260	37	1 " 72,034
Indiana	1,680,637	23	1 " 73,506
Illinois	2,539,891	30	1 " 84,663
Michigan	1,184,059	10	1 " 118,405
Wisconsin	1,054,670	13	1 " 81,128
Total in North-Central States east of the Mississippi	10,445,528	127	1 to 82,249
Missouri	1,721,295	23	1 to 74,839
Iowa	1,194,020	21	1 " 56,858
Minnesota	439,706	3	1 " 146,569
Kansas	364,399	8	1 " 45,550
Nebraska	122,993	4	1 " 30,748
Total in North-Central States west of the Mississippi	3,842,413	59	1 to 65,126
Mississippi	827,922	10	1 to 82,792
Louisiana	726,915	10	1 " 72,691
Arkansas	484,471	5	1 " 96,894
Texas	818,579	12	1 " 68,215
Total in South-Central States	2,857,887	37	1 to 77,240
California	560,247	20	1 to 28,012
Oregon	90,923	9	1 " 10,103
Nevada	42,491	0	....
Colorado	39,864	1	1 to 39,864
Total in Western States	733,525	30	1 to 24,451
Total east of the Mississippi [**]	32,408,217	316	1 to 102,558
Total west of the Mississippi	5,878,938	106	1 " 55,462
Total in the United States	38,287,205	422	1 " 90,728

[*] Census of 1870, excluding "Indians, not taxed."   [**] Including the whole of Louisiana.

CLASSIFICATION OF COLLEGES IN REFERENCE TO CHURCH OR OTHER CONTROL,

Including those whose specific requirements for admission are given.

COLLEGES.	New England States.	Middle States.	South-eastern States.	North-Central States east of the Mississippi.	North-Central States west of the Mississippi.	South-Central States.	Western States.	Total in the United States.
Roman Catholic	2	23	3	15	7	8	9	67
Methodist Episcopal	2	3	5	19	10	4	3	46
South Methodist Episcopal	..	2	7	2	2	2	2	17
Methodist Protestant	..	..	..	1	..	..	..	1
African Methodist Episcopal	..	..	..	1	..	..	..	1
Total Methodist	..	..	..	..	..	..	..	65
Baptist	2	6	7	10	8	7	4	44
Free Baptist	1	..	..	..	..	..	..	1
Seventh-day Baptist	..	1	..	2	..	..	..	3
Free-will Baptist	..	1	..	2	..	..	..	3
Total Baptist	..	..	..	..	..	..	..	51
Presbyterian	..	8	9	9	2	2	..	30
United Presbyterian	..	2	..	3	1	..	..	6
Cumberland Presbyterian	..	1	2	1	..	2	..	6
Southern Presbyterian	..	..	..	1	1	..	..	2
Total Presbyterian	..	..	..	..	..	..	..	44
Congregationalist	6	1	..	9	8	1	..	25
Protestant Episcopal	2	5	2	3	3	..	1	16
Lutheran	..	5	3	6	2	1	..	17
Christian	..	1	1	8	2	..	3	15
Universalist	1	1	..	3	..	..	..	5
United Brethren	..	1	..	3	2	..	1	7
Unitarian	..	..	..	1	1	..	..	2
Friends	..	2	..	2	1	..	..	5
German Reformed	..	3	..	..	..	..	..	3
Reformed (Dutch)	..	2	..	3	..	..	..	5
Congregationalist and Presbyter'n	..	..	..	1	..	..	..	1
Moravian	..	1	..	..	..	..	..	1
New Church	..	..	..	1	..	..	..	1
Jewish	..	..	..	1	..	..	..	1
Evangelical Association	..	..	..	1	..	..	1	2
Masonic	..	..	..	..	..	1	..	1
City	..	1	..	..	..	..	..	1
State Universities	..	6	5	6	5	2	3	27
Non-sectarian	4	15	13	9	2	4	1	48
Unknown	..	..	1	4	2	3	2	12
Total	20	91	58	127	59	37	30	422

HARVARD UNIVERSITY EXAMINATION FOR WOMEN.

ALTHOUGH Harvard University has not opened its doors to women, for class recitation and regular matriculation, it has, nevertheless, following the examples of the English universities, practically expressed its entire accord with the increasing sentiment in favor of the higher education of women, by establishing a system of examinations, under the supervision of its faculty, the details of which, since they are not generally understood, especially among young lady students, we give below, taken from the circular for 1879.

These examinations were held for the first time in 1874, in Boston. The sixth examination will be held simultaneously in Cambridge, New York, Philadelphia, and Cincinnati, beginning at some date between May 27 and June 5, 1879, and will be of two grades: 1. A general or preliminary examination for young women who are not less than seventeen years old; 2. An advanced examination for those who have passed the preliminary examination, and are not less than eighteen years old.

I. PRELIMINARY EXAMINATION.

The Preliminary Examination embraces the following subjects: English, Physical Geography, either Elementary Botany or Elementary Physics, Arithmetic, Algebra through quadratic equations, Plane Geometry, History, and any two of the four languages — French, German, Latin, and Greek — at least one of the two chosen being a modern language.

This examination can be taken as a whole only by young women who are at least seventeen years old. It may, however, at the option of the candidate, be divided between two years; and, in this case, the minimum age of admission is sixteen years. No candidate will, in any case, be admitted to examination on a part of any subject; and no account will be made of a partial examination, unless the candidate has passed satisfactorily in at least three subjects. If the candidate passes in three or more subjects, the results of the partial examination will be recorded by the university; but no certificate will be given until the whole examination has been passed. Candidates who divide the Preliminary Examination will be expected to attain a somewhat higher degree of excellence than those who present the nine subjects at once.

ENGLISH.

Candidates will be examined upon the history of English literature, and be required to write a short composition upon a subject to be given out at the time of examination.

In 1879, the subject will be Shakespeare's *Hamlet* and *Midsummer-Night's Dream,* as edited for the Clarendon Press series by William Aldis Wright.

In 1880, *Macbeth* and *Henry V.* Candidates should consult Abbott's "Shakesperian Grammar" and be able to give a succinct account of the life and works of Chaucer, Spenser, Shakespeare, Bacon, Herbert, Herrick, Milton, Bunyan, Dryden, Addison, Defoe, Pope, Gray, Goldsmith, Johnson, Burke, Burns, Cowper, Jane Austen, Shelley, Byron, Scott, Coleridge, Maria Edgeworth, Wordsworth.

PHYSICAL GEOGRAPHY.

A good knowledge of the ordinary school-books on this subject should be secured. Candidates may also use to advantage Guyot's "Earth and Man," Ritter's "Comparative Geography," and other similar books.

ELEMENTARY PHYSICS.

Balfour Stewart's "Elementary Physics," Ganot's "Elements," may be used for reference.

BOTANY.

Gray's "School and Field Botany" and "How Plants Behave." Each candidate will be required to submit a list of fifty species, of different genera, which she has studied and determined, and also to fill up three schedules with a description of three plants accompanying the schedules.

MATHEMATICS.

Arithmetic, Algebra, and Geometry, entire.

HISTORY.

History of England as far as the year 1689. Such books as Bright's "History of England" (first two volumes) and Green's "History of the

English people" will be of value for reading and study; a familiarity with Geography and Chronology is indispensable.

FRENCH.

The candidate must be able to read French fluently and with a fair pronunciation. Knapp's or Fasquelle's or Otto's French Grammar will serve to indicate the grammatical knowledge demanded. No books are prescribed; but those enumerated below will be sufficient to show the vocabulary and character of the French which candidates should be able to read.

1. Voltaire, "Charles XII." 2. George Sand, "La famille de Germandre." 3. Alfred de Vigny, "Cinq Mars." 4. Sandeau, "Mlle. de la Seiglière" (comedy). 5. Molière, "Le Misanthrope." 6. Racine, "Athalie."

GERMAN.

Candidates will be expected to pronounce the language with reasonable correctness. No books are prescribed; but all are advised to read the following: the introduction to Dr. Buchheim's "Deutsche Lyrik," together with some of the poems in the work itself, and also these:

Zschokke: Der zerbrochene Krug; Das Wirthshaus zu Cransac.

Gerstäcker; Germelshausen.

Paul Heyse: La Rabbiata; Die Blinden.

Theodore Müggo: Signa die Seterin.

Adelbert Stifter: Brigitta.

Schiller: Wilhelm Tell.

Lessing: Minna van Barnhelm.

Goethe: Hermann und Dorothea.

LATIN.

Candidates will be examined upon
1. Latin Grammar and Writing Latin.
2. Caesar, first three books: Nepos, Lives of Miltiades, Themistocles, Aristides, Alcibiades, Epaminondas, Hannibal.
3. The first three books of Virgil's Aeneid.

Ability to read Latin as Latin with accuracy and confidence is desirable.

In reading Latin, the aim should be not only to put the accent in the right place, but to give every syllable its due quantity; for instance, to sound mēmŏriă in such a way that the ear may readily detect a succession of short syllables; to sound the u in lūx (lúcis) long, in dūx (dúcis) short; o long in consul, confido, short in contra; to let i be heard in infans, i in indoctus, e in dēns, e in dēntis, etc., etc.

At all events, an accurate knowledge of the quantity of the penultimate syllable of polysyllabic words is indispensable. Such mispronunciations as arbŏris, arbŭtus, tempŏria, dolŏris, gladiŏlus,

enimtēro, imprŏbus, metuēret are unpardonable. Care must be taken to distinguish words which look alike or nearly alike to the eye; and Latin words which have derivatives in English must especially be looked at with suspicion.

The Roman pronunciation is recommended.

Besides an acquaintance with the outlines of Roman History, some knowledge of Roman Antiquities and of manners and customs is necessary, as well as an acquaintance with the leading events of the period in which the writer who is studied belongs.

GREEK.

Candidates will be examined:
1. Either (A.) in the translation at sight of easy passages of Xenophon (suited to the proficiency of those who have studied the first 111 pages of Goodwin's Greek Reader), with a vocabulary of the less usual words; or (B.) in the first 111 pages of Goodwin's Reader and Book I. of the Iliad, with questions on the subject-matter, and on constructions and grammatical forms.
2. Also, in the translation into Greek of simple sentences, such as those in the first 51 lessons of White's First Lessons in Greek, to test the candidates' practical knowledge of grammar.

Attention to Greek History is strongly recommended. At least some compendium, like Smith's smaller History, should be read; but all who have the needed time and the taste are advised to read the chapters of Grote which illustrate the different parts of their studies.

II. ADVANCED EXAMINATION.

The Advanced Examination is for young women who have passed the Preliminary Examination, and who are not less than eighteen years old. It is divided into five sections, in one or more of which the candidate may present herself. These sections are as follows:

1. Languages.—Candidates may offer any two of the following languages: English, French, German, Italian, Latin, Greek.
2. Physical Science.—Candidates may offer any two of the following subjects: Chemistry, Physics, Botany, Mineralogy, Geology.
3. Mathematics.—Candidates must present Solid Geometry, Algebra, Logarithms, and Plane Trigonometry, and one of the three following subjects: Analytic Geometry, Mechanics, Spherical Trigonometry, and Astronomy.
4. History.—In 1879, candidates may offer either of the two following subjects: 1. The History of Continental Europe during the period of the Reformation, 1517–1648; 2. English and American History from 1688 to the end of the eighteenth century.

5. *Philosophy.*—Candidates may offer any three of the following subjects: Mental Philosophy, Moral Philosophy, Logic, Rhetoric, Political Economy.

FORMS OF CERTIFICATES TO BE GIVEN BY THE UNIVERSITY.

HARVARD UNIVERSITY.

PRELIMINARY EXAMINATION FOR WOMEN.

A—— B—— has passed (passed with distinction) (passed with the highest distinction) the Preliminary Examination, held at ——, on the —— of ——, 187 , under the direction of the Faculty of Harvard University, and is **entitled to** proceed to the Advanced Examination.

—— ——,
President.

CAMBRIDGE, *August* 1, 187 .

HARVARD UNIVERSITY.

ADVANCED EXAMINATION FOR WOMEN.

A—— B——, having duly passed the Preliminary Examination on the —— of ——, 187 , has been admitted to the Advanced Examination in the section (sections) of ——, and has passed (passed with distinction) (passed with the highest distinction) the prescribed examinations in ——, held at ——, under the direction of the Faculty of Harvard University, on the —— of ——, 187 .

—— ——,
President.

CAMBRIDGE, *August* 1, 187 .

Notice of **intention to be candidates must be** sent to the Secretary of **the** Woman's Educational Association, **114** Boylston Street, Boston, **or to** the Secretary **of** the New York Local **Committee,** **59** East Twenty-fifth Street, New York, **or to the** Secretary of the Philadelphia Local **Committee,** **401 South Eighth Street,** Philadelphia, **before April 1, 1879.**[**]

[**] These examinations will be continued from year to year, and candidates should govern themselves accordingly.

Candidates for the Preliminary Examination must specify which of the elective studies (Botany or Physics, and German, Latin, or Greek) they will take. Candidates for the Advanced Examination must specify which section and which subjects they elect.

Exact notice of the place of the examination, and also of the time (day and hour), will be sent to all candidates on April 15, 1879.

The Preliminary Examination will cover parts of two weeks. Less time will be required for the Advanced Examination, according to the number of subjects chosen.

The fee for the Preliminary Examination, including certificate, will be *fifteen dollars.*

The fee for the Advanced Examination will be *ten dollars.*

The Woman's Educational Association and the Local Committees will provide board and lodging at moderate cost for those who need such accommodation.

Young women in narrow circumstances will be aided in meeting the cost of these examinations. Applicants for such aid should address the Secretary of the Educational Association or the Secretary of the Local Committee, stating their circumstances fully—the amount of help they need, the kind of assistance they would prefer, whether a remission of fees, a loan, or gratuitous board and lodging, during the examination—and inclosing certificates of scholarship and character from their teachers.

If an applicant is under twenty-one years of age, her application must be accompanied by the written approval of her parent or guardian.

A pamphlet has been printed containing full lists of books and specimen examination-papers. Copies will be forwarded to any address upon the receipt of twenty-five cents, and any further information that may be desired will be gladly furnished by the Secretary of the Woman's Educational Association, 114 Boylston Street, Boston, Massachusetts, or by the Secretary of the New York Local Committee, 59 East Twenty-fifth Street, New York, or by the Secretary of the Philadelphia Local Committee, 401 South Eighth Street, Philadelphia, or by Professor Charles F. Dunbar, Dean of College Faculty, Cambridge, Mass.

EXAMINATION QUESTIONS FOR ADMISSION TO COLLEGE.

An erroneous impression prevails among many students, that colleges do not insist upon all their requirements for admission; that students may apply with a poor or half preparation, and still be admitted.

To dispel this illusion, and to encourage thorough preparation, which alone renders college life the most fruitful in profit, interest, and pleasure, we give below some specimen sets of questions recently used.

In comparison with others, they are only of average difficulty.

YALE COLLEGE.

English Grammar.

1. How is the comparison of adjectives affected by their number of syllables?

2. Compare the following: Bad; Little; Many; Much; Near.

3. Give an example of the independent construction and of the absolute construction of nouns.

4. Explain the use of the dative-objective case of nouns, and give examples.

5. Give the principal parts of the following irregular verbs: Abide; Awake; Be; Bring; Lie; Ring; Sink; Spit; Stride; Tread; Win.

Analyze the following sentence: Events which, if they ever happened, happened in ages and nations so remote that the particulars never could have been known to him, are related with the greatest minuteness of detail."

Parse the words in italics, giving full particulars of voice, mood, tense and agreement of the verbs.

Geography.

1. Name the countries and larger islands which lie in the Southern Temperate Zone.

2. Name the principal divisions of South America.

3. Describe the relative situation of Australia, Tasmania, Borneo, Papua, New Zealand.

4. Bound the State of Georgia.

5. Locate Sacramento, Prague, Seville, Lima, Ghent, Basle, Warsaw, Lake St. Clair, the Island of Java, the Isle of Man, Cape Comorin, the two capes Sable.

6. Name the principal rivers of England and Spain.

Arithmetic.

1. Add $\frac{3\frac{1}{4}}{6\frac{1}{4}}$ to $\frac{1}{3}$ of $\frac{1}{4}\frac{2}{3}$ of $\frac{2}{3}$ of $(\frac{2}{3}-\frac{1}{4})$.

2. Multiply 903.14 by .063 and extract the square root of the product to three decimal places.

3. Divide 6 by .089 and extract the cube root of the quotient to two decimal places.

4. What is the value, at $4,500 per acre, of a piece of ground containing 30 rd., 19 ft., 89 in.?

5. How many litres in a box 1.2ᵐ long, 8ᵈᵐ wide, and 50ᵐᵐ deep?

Algebra.

1. Find the value of each of the following expressions:

(a) $\frac{1-x^3}{1+y} \times \frac{1-y^3}{x+x^3} \times \left(1+\frac{x}{1-x}\right)$;

(b) $(a^{-2}-a^{\frac{2}{3}})^2$;

(c) $3\sqrt{\frac{1}{3}} + 2\sqrt{1\frac{1}{3}} + 4\sqrt{\frac{1}{12}}$.

2. (a) $\frac{1}{x}+\frac{1}{y}-\frac{1}{z}=a; \frac{1}{x}-\frac{1}{y}+\frac{1}{z}=b; -\frac{1}{x}+\frac{1}{y}+\frac{1}{z}=c$; find x, y, and z.

(b) Solve the equation:
$\frac{17-3x}{5} - \frac{4x+2}{3} = 5 - \left(6x - \frac{7x+14}{3}\right)$

3. Solve the equations:

(a) $\frac{10}{x} - \frac{10}{x+1} = \frac{3}{x+2}$.

(b) $2x^{\frac{2}{3}} + 3x^{\frac{1}{3}} = 2$.

4. (a) Find the sum of 13 terms of the series $2\frac{1}{4}, 2\frac{3}{4}, 3\frac{1}{4}$, etc.

(b) Find the value of $1 + \frac{1}{4} + \frac{1}{16} + \frac{1}{64}$ etc., to infinity.

5. By the binomial theorem expand to five terms $(a^3 + x^3)^{-\frac{2}{3}}$.

Latin Grammar.

[In writing Latin words, mark the quantity of the penult in each.]

1. Write the genitive singular of *frigus*, *virus*, *nemus*, *limen*, and the nominative singular of *salutem*, *sitim*, *litore*, *silicis*, *vulnera*, *aethere*, *sulcis*.

2. Give the gender.of the same nouns.

3. Write out in full the declension of *aliquis*, *ingens*, *exsul*, *hic*.

4. Compare *magnus, tristis*, *malus, nequam*, *proximus*.

5. The principal parts of the verbs from which the following forms are derived: *tenebat, audebat, cernimus, bibet, labatur, haerent*.

6. Inflect the future indicative active of *nosco* and *debeo*, and the present and perfect subjunctive of *morior* and *possum*.

7. Write out in full the conjugation of *fero* in the active voice.

8. What parts of the verb are formed from the perfect stem?

Latin.

Translate into Latin—

1. The rule (*regula*) of expediency (*utilitas*) is the same as that of honor.

2. He told many falsehoods (*mentior*) about his age, that he might seem younger.

3. There were some who denied that virtue and vice were contrary to each other.

4. The business which you promised to finish (*conficio*) has not yet been finished.

5. That you may be able to die courageously live virtuously.

6. What difference does it make (*interest*) whether the Romans conquered or were conquered?

7. On the top of the mountains the cold (*frigus*) is so great, that the snow (*nix*) never melts (*liquesco*) there.

8. He says that he has done good (*prosum*) to very many.

1. Virg. Aen., II. 437–444.

Hic vero ingentem pugnam, ceu cetera nusquam
Bella forent, nulli tota morerentur in urbe,
Sic Martem indomitum Danaosque ad tecta ru-
    entes
Cernimus, obsessamque acta testudine limen.
Haerent parietibus scalae, postesque sub ipsos
Nituntur gradibus, clipeosque ad tela sinistris
Protecti objiciunt, prensant fastigia dextris.

2. (*a*) Why is *forent* subjunctive? How was a *testudo* formed? (*b*) Distinguish between *paries* and *moenia, tela* and *arma*. (*c*) Who were called *Danai?* By what other names does Virgil designate them?

3. (*a*) Divide lines 4 and 5 into feet, marking the quantity of each syllable. (*b*) In this passage, what final syllables having a short vowel are made

long by position? (*c*) Mark the quantity of each syllable in *diei, ab, pacis, dabamus*.

[6 may be substituted for 4 or 5.]

4. Virg. Ecl., I. 59–63.

Ante leves ergo pascentur in aethere cervi,
Et freta destituent nudos in litore pisces,
Ante, pererratis amborum finibus, exsul
Aut Ararim Parthus bibet, aut Germania Tigrim,
Quam nostro illius labatur pectore vultus.

Locate the rivers mentioned in line 4. Distinguish between *lēvis* and *lĕvis*.

5. Virg. Geor., I. 129–135.

Ille malum virus serpentibus addidit atris,
Praedarique lupos jussit, pontumque moveri,
Mellaque decussit foliis, ignemque removit,
Et passim rivis currentia vina repressit,
Ut varias usus meditando extunderet artes
Paulatim, et sulcis frumenti quaereret herbam,
Ut silicis venis abstrusum excuderet ignem.

6. Ovid. Met., III. 55–62.

Ut nemus intravit, letataque corpora vidit,
Victoremque supra spatiosi corporis hostem
Tristia sanguinea lambentem vulnera lingua,
' Aut ultor vestrae, fidissima corpora, mortis,
Aut comes,' inquit, ' ero.' Dixit, dextraque mo-
    larem
Sustulit, et magnum magno conamine misit.
Illius impulsu cum turribus ardua celsis
Moenia mota forent : serpens sine vulnere mansit.

1. Cic. Cat., I. 6.

Quod ego praetermitto et facile patior sileri, ne in hac civitate tanti facinoris immanitas aut exstitisse aut non vindicata esse videatur. Praetermitto ruinas fortunarum tuarum, quas omnes impendere tibi proximis Idibus senties: ad illa venio, quae non ad privatam ignominiam vitiorum tuorum, non ad domesticam tuam difficultatem ac turpitudinem, sed ad summam rem publicam atque ad omnium nostrum vitam salutemque pertinent.

2. (*a*) Explain the subjunctive *videatur*.

(*b*) What days of the months were the Kalends, the Nones, and the Ides? How were the days numbered from these points? Express in Latin *October 21st*.

3. Cic. Cat., III. 7.

Omnia norat, omnium aditus tenebat; appellare, temptare, sollicitare, poterat, audebat ; erat ei consilium ad facinus aptum, consilio autem neque manus neque lingua deerat. Jam ad certas res conficiendas certos homines delectos ac descriptos habebat ; neque vero, cum aliquid mandarat, confectum putabat : nihil erat quod non ipse obiret, occurreret, vigilaret, laboraret ; frigus, sitim, famem ferre poterat.

4. (*a*) Where are the forms *norat* and *poterat* found? Construction of *ei, consilio*. Explain the form *sitim*.

(*b*) What is *asyndeton?* Give an example from this passage.

5. Cic. Arch., I.

Quod si haec vox, hujus hortatu praeceptisque conformata, nonnullis aliquando saluti fuit, a quo id accepimus quo ceteris opitulari et alios servare possemus, huic profecto ipsi, quantum est situm in nobis, et opem et salutem ferro debemus.

6. (a) Give the antecedents of *a quo*, and of *quo*.

(b) What was the charge against Archias? What claim had he to Cicero's services?

Greek.

[Any two of the passages may be omitted.]

1. Xen. An., I. 5, 8.

ἐνθα δὴ μέρος τι τῆς εὐταξίας ἦν θεάσασθαι. ῥίψαν-
τες γὰρ τοὺς πορφυροὺς κάνδυς ὅπου ἔτυχεν ἕκαστος
ἑστηκώς, ἵεντο ὥσπερ ἂν δράμοι τις περὶ νίκης καὶ μάλα
κατὰ πρανοῦς γηλόφου, ἔχοντες τούτους τε τοὺς πολυτε-
λεῖς χιτῶνας καὶ τὰς ποικίλας ἀναξυρίδας, ἔνιοι δὲ καὶ
στρεπτοὺς περὶ τοῖς τραχήλοις καὶ ψέλια περὶ ταῖς χερ-
σίν· εὐθὺς δὲ σὺν τούτοις εἰσπηδήσαντες εἰς τὸν
πηλὸν θᾶττον ἢ ὥς τις ἂν ᾤετο μετεώρους ἐξεκόμισαν τὰς
ἁμάξας.

Give the present of δράμοι, the comparison of θᾶττον. Explain the euphonic changes in θᾶττον. Point out the predicate adjective in this sentence.

2. Xen. An., II. 5, 16.

ἀλλ' ἥδομαι μέν, ὦ Κλέαρχε, ἀκούων σου φρονίμους
λόγους· ταῦτα γὰρ γιγνώσκων εἰ τι ἐμοὶ κακὸν βουλεύοις,
ἅμα ἂν μοι δοκεῖς καὶ σαυτῷ κακόνους εἶναι. ὡς δ' ἂν
μάθῃς, ὅτι οὐδ' ἂν ὑμεῖς δικαίως οὔτε βασιλεῖ οὔτ' ἐμοὶ
ἀπιστοίητε, ἀντάκουσον. εἰ γὰρ ὑμᾶς ἐβουλόμεθα ἀπο-
λέσαι, πότερά σοι δοκοῦμεν ἱππέων πλήθους ἀπορεῖν ἢ
πεζῶν ἢ ὁπλίσεως;

What use of the participle is seen in ἀκούων? To what does ἂν (the one after ἅμα) belong? Construction of μοι, of κακόνους, and of πλήθους?

3. Xen. An., III. 2, 9.

τοῦτο δὲ λέγοντος αὐτοῦ πτάρνυταί τις· ἀκούσαντες
δ' οἱ στρατιῶται πάντες μιῇ ὁρμῇ προσεκύνησαν τὸν θεόν,
καὶ Ξενοφῶν εἶπε, Δοκεῖ μοι ὦ ἄνδρες, ἐπεὶ περὶ σωτη-
ρίας ἡμῶν λεγόντων, οἰωνὸς τοῦ Διὸς τοῦ σωτῆρος ἐφάνη,
εὔξασθαι τῷ θεῷ τούτῳ θύσειν σωτήρια ὅπου ἂν πρῶτον
εἰς φιλίαν χώραν ἀφικώμεθα, συνεπεύξασθαι δὲ καὶ τοῖς
ἄλλοις θεοῖς θύσειν κατὰ δύναμιν. καὶ ὅτῳ δοκεῖ ταῦτ',
ἔφη, ἀνατεινάτω τὴν χεῖρα. καὶ ἀνέτειναν ἅπαντες. ἐκ
τούτου εὔξαντο καὶ ἐπαιάνισαν.

Reason for the subjunctive in ἀφικώμεθα. Construction of ἡμῶν. Construction of the antecedent of ὅτῳ.

4. Xen. An., IV. 4, 15.

ἐντεῦθεν ἔπεμψαν νυκτὸς Δημοκράτην Τεμενίτην ἄν-
δρας δόντες ἐπὶ τὰ ὄρη, ἔνθα ἔφασαν οἱ ἀποσκεδαννύμενοι

καθορᾶν τὰ πυρά· οὗτος γὰρ ἐδόκει καὶ πρότερον πολλὰ
ἤδη ἀληθεῦσαι τοιαῦτα, τὰ ὄντα τε ὡς ὄντα καὶ τὰ μὴ
ὄντα ὡς οὐκ ὄντα. πορευθεὶς δὲ τὰ μὲν πυρὰ οὐκ ἔφη
ἰδεῖν, ἄνδρα δὲ συλλαβὼν ἧκεν ἄγων ἔχοντα τόξον Περ-
σικὸν καὶ φαρέτραν καὶ σάγαριν, οἷάνπερ αἱ Ἀμαζόνες
ἔχουσιν. ἐρωτώμενος δὲ τὰ ποδαπὸς εἴη, Πέρσης μὲν
ἔφη εἶναι, πορεύεσθαι δ' ἀπὸ τοῦ Τιριβάζου στρατεύμα-
τος, ὅπως ἐπιτήδεια λάβοι.

Construction of νυκτός. To what does τό belong? Reason for the optative in εἴη and in
λάβοι.

5. Plato Apol. Soc.

καὶ γὰρ ἐν ταῖς μάχαις πολλάκις δῆλον γίγνεται ὅτι
τό γε ἀποθανεῖν ἄν τις ἐκφύγοι καὶ ὅπλα ἀφεὶς καὶ ἐφ'
ἱκετείαν τραπόμενος τῶν διωκόντων· καὶ ἄλλαι μηχαναί
εἰσιν ἐν ἑκάστοις τοῖς κινδύνοις ὥστε διαφεύγειν θάνατον,
ἐάν τις τολμᾷ πᾶν ποιεῖν καὶ λέγειν. ἀλλὰ μὴ οὐ τοῦτ'
ᾖ χαλεπόν, ὦ ἄνδρες, θάνατον ἐκφυγεῖν, ἀλλὰ πολὺ
χαλεπώτερον πονηρίαν· θᾶττον γὰρ θανάτου θεῖ. καὶ
νῦν ἐγὼ μέν, ἅτε βραδὺς ὢν καὶ πρεσβύτης, ὑπὸ τοῦ
βραδυτέρου ἑάλων, οἱ δ' ἐμοὶ κατήγοροι, ἅτε δεινοὶ καὶ
ὀξεῖς ὄντες, ὑπὸ τοῦ θάττονος, τῆς κακίας.

What shows the mode of τολμᾷ? What is understood before μή? Construction of χαλεπώτερον
and of πονηρίαν. Present of ἑάλων.

Greek History.

1. What is known of Miltiades, of Kleon, of Aratus?

2. Who were the chief men in Greek poli-
tics, philosophy, and art between 400 and 300
B. C.?

3. What are the prominent points in the history of Syracuse?

Greek Grammar and Composition.

[All Greek words are to be written with the accent.]

1. Decline throughout γλῶσσα, λόγος, πατήρ, and
the pronouns τις and οὗτος.

2. Give the synopsis (i. e. first form in every
mode) of the future active and middle of στέλλω,
and of the perfect middle of φαίνω.

3. Analyze λύσομαι, stating where this form is
made.

4. What is the difference of meaning between
εἰσι and εἰσί, ὧν and ὄν, ὁ αὐτὸς ἄνθρωπος and ὁ ἄνθρωπος αὐτός?

5. Translate into Greek—

His mother sends for him from the province
which he holds.

When he had halted[61] his chariot before the
phalanx, he sent for Menon to come to him.

If any one had gone into the city, what would
he have suffered?

[61] Express " when he had halted " by a participle.

BOSTON UNIVERSITY.

Algebra.

1. Remove the parentheses from $-a + m -$ $\{-c + x - [a - m - (c - x)]\}$, and reduce the result to its simplest form.

2. Factor $a^2 z - 3 a^5 x^2$ and $121 m^4 - 100 n^3$.

3. Find the least common multiple of $x^2 + xy$, $xy - y^2$, and $x^2 - y^2$.

4. Add $\dfrac{a}{a+c}, \dfrac{2c}{a-c}, \dfrac{c}{a+c}$.

5. Solve the equations $\begin{cases} x + y - z = 1 \\ 8x + 3y - 6z = 1 \\ 3x - 4z - y = 1 \end{cases}$

6. Extract the cube root of $27 a^3 + 108 a^2 + 144 a + 64$.

7. Solve the equation:
$$x + a = \sqrt[4]{a^2 + z\sqrt{b^3 + z^2}}.$$

Geometry.

1. If the opposite sides of a quadrilateral are equal, each to each, the equal sides are parallel, and the figure is a parallelogram.

2. If four quantities are proportional, the sum of the first and second is to their difference, as the sum of the third and fourth is to their difference.

3. The diameter which is perpendicular to a chord bisects the chord and also the arc which it subtends.

4. The area of a trapezoid is equal to the product of its altitude by half the sum of its parallel sides.

5. In any right-angled triangle, the square described on the hypothenuse is equivalent to the sum of the squares described on the other two sides.

Caesar, Second Book.

1. Translate the following:

Caesar honōris Divitiāci atque Aeduōrum causā sese eos in fidem receptūrum et conservatūrum dixit; sed quod erat civitas magna inter Belgas auctoritāte, atque homĭnum multitudĭne praestābat, sexcentos obsĭdes poposcit. His traditis omnibus- que armis ex oppĭdo collātis, ab eo loco in fines Ambianōrum pervēnit, qui se suāque omnia sine mora dedidērunt. Eōrum fines Nervii attingēbant; quorum de natūra moribusque Caesar quum quae- rēret, sic reperiēbat nullam adĭtam esse ad eos mercatorĭbus: nihil pati vini reliquarumque rerum ad luxuriam pertinentium inferri, quod ĭlis rebus relanguescĕre animos et remittī virtūtem existimā- rent; esse homĭnes feros magnaeque virtūtis: in- crepĭtāre atque incusāre relinquos Belgas, qui se popŭlo Romāno dedidissent patriamque virtūtem projecissent: confirmāre, sese neque legātos mis- sūros, neque ullam conditiōnem pacis acceptūros.

2. To what age of Roman literature does Cae- sar belong? and say what you can of him.

---

3. Locate the tribes named in this section.

4. Parse words in second line.

Prose and Grammar.

1. Forms for expressing time.

2. I had scarcely read your letter when Cur- tius came to me.

3. Discuss (a) Tenses of participles, (b) Use of participles.

4. The Belgians, influenced by the love of glory and relying upon their valor, waged many wars with the Germans.

5. Synonymes for temple; wall; battle.

6. In the consulship of Lucius Cassius, the Hel- vetians routed the Roman army, and sent it under the yoke.

7. Forms for expressing concession.

Aeneid, Book III.

1. Translate the following:

Tendunt vela Noti: fugimus spumantibus undis,
Qua cursum ventusque gubernatorque vocabat.
Jam medio apparet fluctu nemoroso Zacynthos,
Dulichiumque, Sameque, et Neritos ardua saxis.
Effugimus scopulos Ithacae, Laërtia regna,
Et terram altricem saevi exsecramur Ulixi.
Mox et Leucatae nimbosa cacumina montis,
Et formidatus nautis aperitur Apollo.
Hunc petimus fessi, et parvae succedimus urbi:
Ancora de prora jacitur, stant litore puppes.
Ergo insperata tandem tellure potiti,
Lustramurque Jovi, votisque incendimus aras,
Actiaque Iliacis celebramus litora ludis.
Exercent patrias oleo labente palaestras
Nudati socii: juvat evasisse tot urbes
Argolicas, mediosque fugam tenuisse per hostes.

2. What kind of a poem is the Aeneid, when written, and in what measure?

3. Give the story of first six books.

4. Locate Zacynthos, Dulichium, Same, Neritos, and Ithaca.

5. Say what you can of Ulixes, Apollo, and Jupiter.

6. Mark scanning of first four verses.

7. Give rules of quantity first verse.

8. Synopsis of first five verbs (same person and number as in text).

9. Parse qua, nautis, tellure, and evasisse.

10. Derivation of gubernator, altricem, potiti, and Greek for Jupiter, Ulixes, urbes, and qua.

11. Name places visited by Aeneas in the jour- ney from Troy to Italy. How many years do the events of this book cover?

Cicero—Oration III. against Catiline.

1. Translate the following:

Ac ne longum sit, Quirites, tabellas proferri jussimus quae a quoque dicebantur datae. Primum ostendimus Cethego signum : cognovit. Nos linum incidimus: legimus. Erat scriptum ipsius manu Allobrogum senatui et populo, sese quae eorum legatis confirmasset facturum esse; orare ut item illi facerent quae sibi eorum legati recepissent. Tum Cethegus, qui paulo ante aliquid tamen de gladiis ac sicis, quae apud ipsum erant deprehensa, respondisset, dixissetque se semper bonorum ferramentorum studiosum fuisse, recitatis litteris debilitatus atque abjectus conscientia repente conticuit. Introductus est Statilius: cognovit et signum et manum suam. Recitatae sunt tabellae in eandem fere sententiam: confessus est. Tum ostendi tabellas Lentulo, et quaesivi cognosceretne signum. Adnuit.

2. When, where, and why was the third oration delivered ?

3. Explain the word *Quirites* as applied to the Romans.

4. What can you say of *Cethegus, Statilius,* and *Lentulus ?*

5. Derivation of *tabellas, senatui, legatis, ferramentorum,* and *litteris.*

6. Reason for the subjunctives in the above.

7. Parse all the words in first two lines.

8. Greek corresponding to *erat, illi, ipsum,* and *se.*

Greek.

Translate—

Κλέαρχος δ᾽ ἔλεγεν· Ἡμεῖς οὔτε συνήλθομεν ὡς βασιλεῖ πολεμήσοντες οὔτ᾽ ἐπορευόμεθα ἐπὶ βασιλέα· ἀλλὰ πολλὰς προφάσεις Κῦρος εὕρισκεν, ὡς καὶ σὺ εὖ οἶσθα, ἵνα ὑμᾶς τε ἀπαρασκευάστους λάβοι καὶ ἡμᾶς ἐνθάδε ἀναγάγοι. Ἐπεὶ μέντοι ἤδη αὐτὸν ἑωρῶμεν ἐν δεινῷ ὄντα, ᾐσχύνθημεν καὶ θεοὺς καὶ ἀνθρώπους προδοῦναι αὐτόν, ἐν τῷ πρόσθεν χρόνῳ παρέχοντες ἡμᾶς αὐτοὺς εὖ ποιεῖν. Ἐπεὶ δὲ Κῦρος τέθνηκεν, οὔτε βασιλεῖ ἀντιποιούμεθα τῆς ἀρχῆς οὔτ᾽ ἔστιν ὅτου ἕνεκα βουλοίμεθ᾽ ἂν τὴν βασιλέως χώραν κακῶς ποιεῖν· οὐδ᾽ αὐτὸν ἀποκτεῖναι ἂν ἐθέλοιμεν, πορευοίμεθα δ᾽ ἂν οἴκαδε, εἴ τις ἡμᾶς μὴ λυποίη· ἀδικοῦντα μέντοι πειρασόμεθα σὺν τοῖς θεοῖς ἀμύνασθαι· ἐὰν μέντοι τις ἡμᾶς καὶ εὖ ποιῶν ὑπάρχῃ, καὶ τούτου εἴς γε δύναμιν οὐχ ἡττησόμεθα εὖ ποιοῦντες.

1. Give the parts of λέγω, εὑρίσκω, ὁράω, προδίδωμι, and παρέχω.

2. Write the synopsis of λάβοι, προδοῦναι, ἀποκτεῖναι, and λυποίη.

3. State the different kinds of pronouns in this extract.

4. Give the dat. plu. for all the common nouns found here.

5. Inflect σύ, θεός in sing., Κῦρος, ἀρχή in sing. and dual.

6. Write the personal endings of the secondary tenses of the passive voice.

7. Give illustrations of all the kinds of reduplication in the Greek verb.

8 What are the chief uses of the Greek genitive?

9. What reason can you give for the change from the aorist to the imperfect, in lines 1 and 2 ?

10. Translate into Greek—

(*a*) Let us war with the barbarians, but not with our own friends.

(*b*) The bad always find many pretexts not to do what they ought.

(*c*) If we saw you in danger, we should be ashamed not to furnish you money and men.

(*d*) We shall find, as you too know, many citizens wishing to betray both generals and country.

(*e*) Who will tell us for what reason he is wronging the Greeks ?

Translate—

ὃν τινα μὲν βασιλῆα καὶ ἔξοχον ἄνδρα κιχείη,
τὸν δ᾽ ἀγανοῖς ἐπέεσσιν ἐρητύσασκε παραστάς·
"δαιμόνι᾽, οὔ σε ἔοικε κακὸν ὣς δειδίσσεσθαι,
ἀλλ᾽ αὐτός τε κάθησο καὶ ἄλλους ἵδρυε λαούς.
οὐ γάρ πω σάφα οἶσθ᾽ οἷος νόος Ἀτρείωνος·
νῦν μὲν πειρᾶται, τάχα δ᾽ ἴψεται υἷας Ἀχαιῶν.
ἐν βουλῇ δ᾽ οὐ πάντες ἀκούσαμεν οἷον ἔειπεν.
μή τι χολωσάμενος ῥέξῃ κακὸν υἷας Ἀχαιῶν.
θυμὸς δὲ μέγας ἐστὶ διοτρεφέος βασιλῆος,
τιμὴ δ᾽ ἐκ Διός ἐστι, φιλεῖ δέ ἑ μητίετα Ζεύς."
ὃν δ᾽ αὖ δήμου ἄνδρα ἴδοι βοόωντά τ᾽ ἐφεύροι,
τὸν σκήπτρῳ ἐλάσασκεν ὁμοκλήσασκέ τε μύθῳ.

1. Give the name of the agent, the cause, and the purpose of the action here described.

2. Write the synopsis of παραστάς, οἷσθ᾽, ἴδοι, ἐφεύροι.

3. Account for the moods in κιχείη and ῥέξῃ.

4. Compare ἀγανοῖς, κακόν, and μέγας.

5. Inflect ὅντινα in sing. mas., ἄνδρα and αὐτός in sing., οἷσθ᾽ throughout, πάντες in plural, and Ζεύς.

6. What is the construction of ἐπέεσσιν, σε, αὐτός, and οἷος ?

7. Note all the enclitics in the extract.

8. What would you write in Attic prose for βασιλῆα ἐπέεσσιν, διοτρεφέος, ἑ (v. 10) and βοόωντά ?

9. Describe the species of verse before you.

10. Write a scheme for *iambic trimeter acatalectic.*

DARTMOUTH COLLEGE.

United States History.

1. Give a brief account of the French and Indian wars, and the questions settled by them.

2. Benjamin Franklin's work in the Revolution; state the cause, principal events, and results of the war of 1812.

3. Date of the Secession movement; names of states that participated in it; its length, and the issue.

4. Name and define the departments of the United States Government.

English History.

1. Henry the Eighth and the Reformation.

2. The great Revolution and Oliver Cromwell.

3. Principal events in Queen Victoria's reign.

4. Name the distinguishing features of the Government of England.

Geography.

1. Population and area of the United States. Population and area of the New England States.

Where are the coal areas of America?

What does the District of Columbia include, and how is it governed?

2. Government, population, and products of Brazil and Mexico.

3. Give the political divisions of Europe with the capital and chief cities of each; what states are included in the German Empire?

4. Name the divisions of Ancient Greece and the chief cities. What were the possessions of the Carthaginians at the beginning of the First Punic War? Name the provinces embraced in the Roman Empire in the days of Trajan.

Grammar.

1. Give the rules for the formation of the plural of nouns and also for the comparison of adjectives and adverbs.

2. Give the different uses of the word *that*, and illustrate each; what are the forms and uses of the potential mode?

3. Distinguish between a complex and a compound sentence, and illustrate with four sentences —the first two complex and the last two compound.

4. Parse the Italicised words in the following sentence: *Were* he *my own* brother, this hand *would strike* him *dead*.

Correct, explaining the correction: Whom do men say that I am?

Arithmetic.

$\frac{3\frac{1}{2} + 1\frac{1}{2} + \frac{3}{4}}{6\frac{1}{2} - \frac{3}{4} \times \frac{3}{4}} = ?$ What is a fraction? Find the least common multiple and highest common divisor of 8, 12, and 40. Name the metric units of weights and measures. How many metres in 25 feet? Find the cubic root of 3.375.

$1,000 includes a sum to be invested and a commission of five per cent. of the sum to be invested. What is the sum to be invested?

Algebra.

Define term, factor, coefficient, exponent, power, root, equation. What is the degree of a term? What is a polynominal homogeneous?

Write the following without using the radical sign:

$$\sqrt{a}\,; \ \sqrt[3]{a^2}\,; \ \sqrt{a^3 + b^3 - 2ab}.$$

Write the following without using negative exponents:

$$a^{-3}\,; \ ab^{-3}\,; \ \frac{a^{-3}}{b^{-3}}.$$

Multiply $a - b\sqrt{-1}$ by $a + b\sqrt{-1}$. Also $a - b\sqrt{-1}$ by $a + c\sqrt{-1}$.

Raise $a - b\sqrt{-1}$ to the 3d power. Simplify the radical $(a^3 - 2a^2b + ab^2)^{\frac{1}{2}}$.

Solve $\frac{a^2 - x^2}{a + x} \cdot \frac{a^2 - x^2}{a - x} = b$. Also $\frac{a}{x^{-1}} + bx^2$

$+ c = 0$. Also $\frac{x - 1}{2} - \frac{x - 2}{3} = \frac{x + 1}{6}$. Also

$\frac{a\frac{1}{2} - (a - x)\frac{1}{2}}{a\frac{1}{2} + (a - x)\frac{1}{2}} = \frac{1}{a}$

Geometry.

Define line, angle, surface, figure. What are similar figures? Name the classes of quadrilaterals. Prove that two triangles with the three sides of the one equal to the three sides of the other, each to each, are equal. Prove that the three angles of a triangle are equal to two right angles. Prove that the angle made by two chords intersecting in a circle is measured by one half the sum of the arcs intercepted between its sides and the sides of its vertical, or opposite, angle. Prove that, if two chords intersect each other in a circle, their segments are reciprocally proportional.

Latin.

Give general rules for gender of nouns.

Give the regular methods of forming the second and third roots of verbs.

Give the principles that govern the use of the

indicative, subjunctive, and infinitive moods, and illustrate by some Latin examples.

Give the Roman method of expressing dates, both of the year and the month.

Translate idiomatically one of the three following passages:

Caesar, Gallic War, Bk. II. ch. XXV.

XXV. Caesar ab decimae legionis cohortatione ad dextrum cornu profectus, ubi suos urgeri, signisque in unum locum conlatis, duodecimae legionis confertos milites sibi ipsos ad pugnam esse impedimento vidit,—quartae cohortis omnibus centurionibus occisis, signiferoque interfecto, signo amisso, reliquarum cohortium omnibus fere centurionibus aut vulneratis aut occisis, in his primipilo P. Sextio Baculo, fortissimo viro, multis gravibusque vulneribus confecto, ut jam se sustinere non posset: reliquos esse tardiores, et nonnullos ab novissimis deserto proelio excedere ac tela vitare, hostis neque a fronte ex inferiore loco subeuntes intermittere, et ab utroque latere instare, et rem esse in angusto vidit, neque ullum esse subsidium quod summitti posset,—scuto ab novissimis uni militi detracto, quod ipse eo sine scuto venerat, in primam aciem processit; centurionibusque nominatim appellatis, reliquos cohortatus, milites signa inferre et manipulos laxare jussit, quo facilius gladiis uti possent. Cujus adventu spe inlata militibus, ac redintegrato animo, cum pro se quisque in conspectu imperatoris etiam in extremis suis rebus operam navare cuperet, paulum hostium impetus tardatus est.

Sallust, Catilina, ch. XII.

XII. Postquam divitiae honori esse coepere, et eas gloria, imperium, potentia sequebatur, hebescere virtus, paupertas probro haberi, innocentia pro malivolentia duci coepit. Igitur ex divitiis juventutem luxuria atque avaritia cum superbia invasere; rapere, consumere, sua parvi pendere, aliena cupere, pudorem, pudicitiam, divina atque humana promiscua, nihil pensi neque moderati habere. Operae pretium est, quum domos atque villas cognoveris in urbium modum exaedificatas, visere templa deorum, quae nostri maiores, religiosissimi mortales, fecere. Verum illi delubra deorum pietate, domos suas gloria decorabant, neque victis quidquam praeter iniuriae licentiam eripiebant. At hi contra, ignavissumi homines, per summum scelus omnia ea sociis adimere, quae fortissumi viri victores reliquerant; proinde quasi iniuriam facere id demum esset imperio uti.

Sallust, Iugurtha, ch. XXVIII.

XXVIII. At Iugurtha, contra spem nuncio accepto, quippe cui Romae omnia venum ire in animo haeserat, filium et cum eo duos familiares ad Senatum legatos mittit, hisque ut illis, quos, Hiempsale interfecto, miserat, praecepit, omnes mortales pecunia adgrediantur. Qui postquam Romam adventabant, Senatus a Bestia consultus est, placeretne legatos Iugurthae recipi moenibus; iique decrevere, nisi regnum ipsumque deditum venissent, uti in diebus proximis decem Italia decederent. Consul Numidis ex Senati decreto nunciari iubet: ita infectis rebus illi domum discedunt. Interim Calpurnius, parato exercitu, legat sibi homines nobiles, factiosos, quorum auctoritate quae deliquisset munita fore sperabat: in quis fuit Scaurus, cuius de natura et habitu supra memoravimus.

Also translate:

Cicero, Second Oration against Catiline, ch. VIII.

VIII. Sed cur tamdiu de uno hoste loquimur; et de eo hoste, qui jam fatetur se esse hostem; et quem, quia (quod semper volui) murus interest, non timeo; de his, qui dissimulant, qui Romae remanent, qui nobiscum sunt, nihil dicimus? quos quidem ego, si ullo modo fieri possit, non tam ulcisci studeo, quam sanare, et ipsos placare reipublicae; neque, id quare fieri non possit, si me audire volent, intelligo. Exponam enim vobis, Quirites, ex quibus generibus hominum istae copiae comparantur: deinde singulis medicinam consili atque orationis meae, si quam potero, afferam. Unum genus est eorum, qui, magno in aere alieno, majores etiam possessiones habent, quarum amore adducti dissolvi nullo modo possunt. Horum hominum species est honestissima (sunt enim locupletes), voluntas vero et causa impudentissima. Tu agris, tu aedificiis, tu argento, tu familia, tu rebus omnibus ornatus et copiosus sis; et dubites de possessione detrahere, acquirere ad fidem? Quid enim expectas? bellum? quid? ergo in vastatione omnium tuas possessiones sacrosanctas futuras putas? An tabulas novas? errant, qui istas a Catilina expectant. Meo beneficio tabulae novae proferentur, verum auctionariae: neque enim isti, qui possessiones habent, alia ratione ulla salvi esse possunt. Quod si maturius facere voluissent, neque (id quod stultissimum est) certare cum usuris fructibus praediorum; et locupletioribus his et melioribus civibus uteremur. Sed hosce homines minime puto pertimescendos, quod aut deduci de sententia possunt; aut, si permanebunt, magis mihi videntur vota facturi contra rempublicam, quam arma laturi.

Virgil, Georgics, Bk. IV. ll. 507-527.

"Septem illum totos perhibent ex ordine menses
Rupe sub aeria deserti ad Strymonis undam
Flevisse, et gelidis haec evolvisse sub antris,
Mulcentem tigres, et agentem carmine quercus:
Qualis populea maerens Philomela sub umbra
Amissos queritur fetus, quos durus arator
Observans nido implumes detraxit: at illa
Flet noctem, ramoque sedens miserabile carmen
Integrat, et maestis late loca questibus implet.
Nulla Venus, non ulli animum flexere hymenaei;
Solus hyperboreas glacies Tanaimque nivalem,
Arvaque Rhipaeis nunquam viduata pruinis
Lustrabat, raptam Eurydicen atque irrita Ditis
Dona querens: spretae Ciconum quo munere matres
Inter sacra deum nocturnique orgia Bacchi,
Discerptum latos juvenem sparsere per agros.
Tum quoque, marmorea caput a cervice revulsum
Gurgite quum medio portans Oeagrius Hebrus
Volveret, 'Eurydicen' vox ipsa et frigida lingua
'Ah miseram Eurydicen!' anima fugienta vocabat;
'Eurydicen' toto referebant flumine ripae."

Virgil, Aeneid, Book VI. ll. 102-123.

Incipit Aeneas heros: "Non ulla laborum,
O virgo, nova mi facies inopinave surgit:
Omnia praecepi, atque animo mecum ante peregi.
Unum oro—quando hic inferni janua regis
Dicitur, et tenebrosa palus Acheronte refuso—
Ire ad conspectum cari genitoris et ora
Contingat: doceas iter, et sacra ostia pandas.
Illum ego per flammas et mille sequentia tela
Eripui his humeris, medioque ex hoste recepi:

Ille, meum comitatus iter, maria omnia mecum
Atque omnes pelagique minas coelique ferebat
Invalidus, vires ultra sortemque senectae.
Quin, ut te supplex peterem et tua limina adirem,
Idem orans mandata dabat. Natique patrisque,
Alma, precor, miserere; potes namque omnia:
nec te
Nequidquam lucis Hecate praefecit Avernis:
Si potuit manes arcessere conjugis Orpheus,
Threicia fretus cithara fidibusque canoris;
Si fratrem Pollux alterna morte redemit,
Itque reditque viam toties. Quid Thesea, magnum
Quid memorem Alciden? Et mi genus ab Jove
summo."

Mark the quantities of the last three lines.

Locate the following: Rome, Mantua, Arpi-
num, Eryx, Palinurus, Samnium, Campania, Gaul,
Rhodanus, Liger, Garumna.

Translate into Latin:

The noble Brutus hath told you that Caesar
is ambitious. If it were so it were a grievous
(maxima) fault. Walking is pleasanter than rid-
ing, but it strikes me that we should not enter the
wood without taking arms. On the 10th of July
my friend will set out for Italy, then go to Athens,
and then to Syria.

Greek Grammar.

[N. B.—All Greek words must be written with their accents.]

1. Decline τιμή, πολίτης, νῆσος, παῖς, μέγας, αὐτός,
ἐγώ.

2. Compare σοφός, ταχύς, φίλος, ῥᾴδιος.

3. Inflect λύω in Aorist Imperative, Middle
Voice; λείπω in Second Aorist Subjunctive, Mid-
dle Voice; φαίνω in Aorist Indicative, Active
Voice.

4. Describe all the regular forms of conditional
sentence referring to the future. How would you
express a wish which cannot be fulfilled? a purpose which was not carried out?

5. In what different ways can the Greek express "purpose"?

6. What is a palatal? a lingual? a mute?

7. What is Crasis? Elision? Syncope? Aphae-
resis?

8. With verbs of accusing, what construction
is used?

9. Translate ἐμοί τοῦτο μέλει, and explain the
case of τούτου.

Translate one of the three following passages
from Xenophon's Anabasis:

Bk. II. 6, 16–19:

Πρόξενος δὲ ὁ Βοιώτιος εὐθὺς μὲν μειράκιον ὢν ἐπεθύμει
γενέσθαι ἀνὴρ τὰ μεγάλα πράττειν ἱκανός· καὶ διὰ ταύτην
τὴν ἐπιθυμίαν ἔδωκε Γοργίᾳ ἀργύριον τῷ Λεοντίνῳ. ἐπεὶ δὲ
συνεγένετο ἐκείνῳ, ἱκανὸς νομίσας ἤδη εἶναι καὶ ἄρχειν καὶ
φίλος ὢν τοῖς πρώτοις μὴ ἡττᾶσθαι εὐεργετῶν, ἦλθεν εἰς
ταύτας τὰς σὺν Κύρῳ πράξεις· καὶ ᾤετο κτήσεσθαι ἐκ τούτων ὄνομα μέγα καὶ δύναμιν μεγάλην καὶ χρήματα πολλά.
τοσούτων δ᾽ ἐπιθυμῶν σφόδρα ἔνδηλον αὖ καὶ τοῦτο εἶχεν,
ὅτι τούτων οὐδὲν ἂν θέλοι κτᾶσθαι μετὰ ἀδικίας, ἀλλὰ σὺν

τῷ δικαίῳ καὶ καλῷ ᾤετο δεῖν τούτων τυγχάνειν, ἄνευ δὲ
τούτων μή. ἄρχειν δὲ καλῶν μὲν καὶ ἀγαθῶν δυνατὸς ἦν·
οὐ μέντοι οὔτ᾽ αἰδῶ τοῖς στρατιώταις ἑαυτοῦ οὔτε φόβον
ἱκανὸς ἐμποιῆσαι, ἀλλὰ καὶ ᾐσχύνετο μᾶλλον τοὺς στρατιώτας ἢ οἱ ἀρχόμενοι ἐκεῖνον, καὶ φοβούμενος μᾶλλον ἦν φανε-
ρὸς τὸ ἀπεχθάνεσθαι τοῖς στρατιώταις ἢ οἱ στρατιῶται τὸ
ἀπιστεῖν ἐκείνῳ.

Bk. III. 1, 45-47:

Μετὰ δὲ τοῦτον εἶπε Χειρίσοφος, Ἀλλὰ πρόσθεν μέν,
ὦ Ξενοφῶν, τοσοῦτον μόνον σε ἐγίγνωσκον, ὅσον ἤκουον
Ἀθηναῖον εἶναι, νῦν δὲ καὶ ἐπαινῶ σε ἐφ᾽ οἷς λέγεις τε καὶ
πράττεις, καὶ βουλοίμην ἂν ὅτι πλείστους εἶναι τοιούτους·
κοινὸν γὰρ ἂν εἴη τὸ ἀγαθόν. καὶ νῦν, ἔφη, μὴ μέλλωμεν,
ὦ ἄνδρες, ἀλλ᾽ ἀπελθόντες ἤδη αἱρεῖσθε οἱ δεόμενοι ἄρχον-
ται, καὶ ἑλόμενοι ἥκετε εἰς τὸ μέσον τοῦ στρατοπέδου καὶ
τοὺς αἱρεθέντας ἄγετε. ἔπειτ᾽ ἐκεῖ συγκαλοῦμεν τοὺς ἄλλους στρατιώτας. παρέστω δ᾽ ἡμῖν, ἔφη, καὶ Τολμίδης ὁ
κῆρυξ. καὶ ἅμα ταῦτ᾽ εἰπὼν ἀνέστη, ὡς μὴ μέλλοιτο, ἀλλὰ
περαίνοιτο τὰ δέοντα. ἐκ τούτου ᾑρέθησαν ἄρχοντες ἀντὶ
μὲν Κλεάρχου Τιμασίων Δαρδανεύς, ἀντὶ δὲ Σωκράτους
Ξανθικλῆς Ἀχαιός, ἀντὶ δὲ Ἁγίου Κλεάνωρ Ἀρκάς, ἀντὶ δὲ
Μένωνος Φιλήσιος Ἀχαιός, ἀντὶ δὲ Προξένου Ξενοφῶν
Ἀθηναῖος.

Bk. IV. 2, 17–20:

Καὶ ἐν τούτῳ τῷ χρόνῳ ἦλθεν Ἀρχαγόρας ὁ Ἀργεῖος
πεφευγὼς καὶ λέγει ὡς ἀπεκόπησαν ἀπὸ τοῦ πρώτου λόφου
καὶ ὅτι τεθνᾶσι Κηφισόδωρος καὶ Ἀμφικράτης καὶ ἄλλοι
ὅσοι μὴ ἁλλόμενοι κατὰ τῆς πέτρας πρὸς τοὺς ὀπισθοφύλα-
κας ἀφίκοντο. ταῦτα δὲ διαπραξάμενοι οἱ βάρβαροι ἧκον
ἐπ᾽ ἀντίπορον λόφον τῷ μαστῷ· καὶ Ξενοφῶν διελέγετο
αὐτοῖς δι᾽ ἑρμηνέως περὶ σπονδῶν καὶ τοὺς νεκροὺς ἀπῄτει.
οἱ δὲ ἔφασαν ἀποδώσειν ἐφ᾽ ᾧ μὴ καίειν τὰς κώμας. συνω-
μολόγει ταῦτα ὁ Ξενοφῶν. ἐν ᾧ δὲ τὸ μὲν ἄλλο στράτευμα
παρῄει, οἱ δὲ ταῦτα διελέγοντο, πάντες οἱ ἐκ τούτου τοῦ
τόπου συνερρύησαν. ἐνταῦθα ἵσταντο οἱ πολέμιοι. καὶ
ἐπεὶ ἤρξαντο καταβαίνειν ἀπὸ τοῦ μαστοῦ πρὸς τοὺς ἄλλους,
ἵνα τὰ ὅπλα ἔκειντο, ἵεντο δὴ οἱ πολέμιοι πολλῷ πλήθει
καὶ θορύβῳ· καὶ ἐπεὶ ἐγένοντο ἐπὶ τῆς κορυφῆς τοῦ μαστοῦ,
ἀφ᾽ οὗ Ξενοφῶν κατέβαινεν, ἐκυλίνδουν πέτρας· καὶ ἑνὸς
μὲν κατέαξαν τὸ σκέλος, Ξενοφῶντα δὲ ὁ ὑπασπιστὴς ἔχων
τὴν ἀσπίδα ἀπέλιπεν.

Translate both of the following passages from
Homer's "Iliad":

Bk. I. 245–253:

Ὣς φάτο Πηλείδης, ποτὶ δὲ σκῆπτρον βάλε γαίῃ
χρυσείοις ἥλοισι πεπαρμένον, ἕζετο δ᾽ αὐτός·
Ἀτρείδης δ᾽ ἑτέρωθεν ἐμήνιε. τοῖσι δὲ Νέστωρ
ἡδυεπὴς ἀνόρουσε, λιγὺς Πυλίων ἀγορητής,
τοῦ καὶ ἀπὸ γλώσσης μέλιτος γλυκίων ῥέεν αὐδή.
τῷ δ᾽ ἤδη δύο μὲν γενεαὶ μερόπων ἀνθρώπων
ἐφθίαθ᾽, οἵ οἱ πρόσθεν ἅμα τράφεν ἠδ᾽ ἐγένοντο
ἐν Πύλῳ ἠγαθέῃ, μετὰ δὲ τριτάτοισιν ἄνασσεν.

Bk. II. 190–197:

" Δαιμόνι᾽, οὔ σε ἔοικε κακὸν ὣς δειδίσσεσθαι,
ἀλλ᾽ αὐτός τε κάθησο καὶ ἄλλους ἵδρυε λαούς.
οὐ γάρ πω σάφα οἶσθ᾽ οἷος νόος Ἀτρείωνος·
νῦν μὲν πειράται, τάχα δ᾽ ἴψεται υἷας Ἀχαιῶν.
ἐν βουλῇ δ᾽ οὐ πάντες ἀκούσαμεν οἷον ἔειπεν.
μή τι χολωσάμενος ῥέξῃ κακὸν υἷας Ἀχαιῶν."

θυμὸς δὲ μέγας ἐστὶ διοτρεφέος βασιλῆος,
τιμὴ δ' ἐκ Διός ἐστι, φιλεῖ δέ ἑ μητίετα Ζεύς."

Greek Prose Writing.

Translate into Greek:
1. All these soldiers have the same general.
2. They themselves will fight *according to their ability.*[52]

3. The general himself saved entire cities, with the help of the gods.
4. If he is a brother of yours, you will not take these things *without a battle.*[53]

Geography.

Locate the river Eurotas, the Peneus, Taygetus Mountains, Pindus Mountains, Heymettus Mountain. Which is the longest river in Greece?

BOWDOIN COLLEGE.

Arithmetic.

[Time allowed, half an hour.]

1. (a) Add together $21\frac{1}{4}$, $16\frac{2}{3}$, 4, $26\frac{1}{2}$.

(b) Find the value of

$$(\tfrac{4}{5} \times 2\tfrac{1}{2} \div \tfrac{4}{5} + \tfrac{4}{5}) + \tfrac{4}{5}$$

(c) Reduce $\frac{252}{444}$ to its lowest terms.

(d) Change $\frac{11}{12}$ to an equivalent fraction having 671 for its denominator.

2. (a) Reduce $\frac{7}{12}$ to a decimal of 4 places.

(b) Multiply two thousand five hundred and thirty-four millionths by three thousand two hundred and fifty-six hundred thousandths, and divide the product by eighty ten-thousandths.

3. (a) Sold a horse for $132 at a loss of 12 per cent.; what per cent. would have been gained if the horse had been sold for $159?

(b) What is the amount of $575 at 6 per cent. for 2 years, 6 months and 15 days?

4. Find the square root of 45.9684; of 4.59684; of .00001.

Algebra.

[Candidates are expected to answer at least twelve questions. These may be selected at pleasure, two from each section. The time allowed for the examination is one hour and a half.]

1. (1) Find the numerical value of $\sqrt{(b^2 - ac)} + \sqrt{(2ac + c^2)}$ when $a = 6$, $b = 5$, $c = 4$.

(2) Add together $14a^3x - 7a^2b^3 + 3a^2$, $5a^2b^3c^2 + 3a^3b^3 + 2a^2$, $-(5a^3x + a^3 - 2a^2b^2c^2)$, and $4a^3b^3 - (9a^2x + 4a^2)$.

(3) Multiply $2a^3 - 3ab + 4$ by $a^3 + 2ab - 3$.

(4) Divide $40a^3b^3 + 60a^2b^2 - 17ab$ by $-ab$.

2. (5) Find the greatest common divisor of $4a^3 - 2a^2 - 3a + 1$ and $3a^2 - 2a - 1$.

(6) What is the "least common multiple" of two or more quantities?

3. (7) Reduce $\dfrac{14a^3 - 7ab}{10ac - 5bc}$ to its lowest terms.

(8) Reduce $(a - 1)^2 - \dfrac{(a - 1)^3}{a}$ to the form of a fraction.

(9) Add together $\dfrac{a}{2}$, $\dfrac{a - 2m}{4}$, and $\dfrac{a + 2m}{4}$.

(10) Divide $\dfrac{a}{a + b} + \dfrac{b}{a - b}$ by $\dfrac{a}{a - b} - \dfrac{b}{a + b}$.

4. (11) Solve the equation, $3x - \dfrac{8x + 1}{7} = \dfrac{2x + 9}{3} + 4$.

(12) A bookseller sold 10 books at a certain price, and afterward 15 more at the same rate. At the last sale he received $25 more than at the first. What did he receive for each book?

(13)
$$\frac{1}{x} = m - \frac{1}{y}$$
$$\frac{1}{y} = \frac{1}{x} - n.$$

Find x and y.
If $y = 2x$, which is greater, m or n? How much greater?

5. (14) Write $(-4a^3x^{-4}y^2)^{-3}$ without negative exponents.

(15) Find the cube root of $-\dfrac{125a^3b^3x^{15}}{216c^3z^3}$.

(16) Find the square root of $8ab^3 + a^4 - 4a^3b + 4b^4$.

6. (17) What is a "radical quantity"? A "surd"? Give examples.

(18) Write $2a^3bx$ as a radical of the third degree.

(19) Reduce $\sqrt{3}$, $2^{\frac{2}{3}}$ and $2^{\frac{3}{4}}$ to a common index.

(20) Multiply $(3 + \sqrt{5})^{\frac{1}{2}}$ by $(3 - \sqrt{5})^{\frac{3}{2}}$.

(21) Find the square root of $4 + 2\sqrt{3}$.

(22) Solve the equation $\sqrt{(x + 19)} + (x + 10)^{\frac{1}{2}} = 9$.

Geometry.

[Time allowed, one hour.]

1. (a) What is a geometrical figure? Illustrate.

(b) When is one angle the complement of another? The supplement? Illustrate.

(c) Can a right-angled triangle be isosceles? Is a rhombus a parallelogram? Draw a figure of each.

(d) In an obtuse-angled triangle can a perpen-

[52] κατὰ δύναμιν.   [53] ἀμαχεί.

dicular be drawn from each of the angular points to the opposite side? **Illustrate.**

2. Prove this proposition:

If from a point within a triangle two **straight** lines are drawn to the extremities of either **side,** their sum will be less than the **sum of the other** two sides of the triangle.

3. (a) What is a segment of a circle? Illustrate.

(b) Construct the following figure:

Describe a circle; take any point A upon the circumference; draw the diameter A B; take any other point C upon the circumference; join A C and B C.

What is the angle A C B? What is it measured by?

4. Prove this proposition:

The angle formed by **two chords which cut each** other is measured by **one half of the sum of** the arcs intercepted between **its sides and between the** sides of its vertical **angle.**

Latin.

[Write only on one side of the paper. Number the sheets and write your name at the top of each. On the first sheet state the length of time you have given to the study of Latin, and the amount which you have read. Translate II. and III., and either IV. or V.]

I.

1. Inflect *Aeneas, deus, filius* (in sing.), and *vis.*
2. What is the gender of nouns of the fourth and fifth declensions?
3. What is a patronymic?
4. Inflect *qui* and *alius.*
5. Compare the following adjectives and the adverbs derived from them: *audax, bonus, fortis, miser, proximus.*
6. Write the abl. sing. of the following: *felix, levis, melior, senex.* When do you find *a* and when *ia* in the nom. pl. neut. of adjectives?
7. Give a synopsis of *malo* and *capio* through active voice.
8. Give the principal parts of *gaudeo, interficio, lavo, paciscor, tollo.*
9. Inflect *rego* and *audio* in pres. indic., and mark the quantity of the penult.
10. What parts of the verb are formed from the supine **stem?**

II.

Sed quoniam earum rerum quas ego gessi non eadem est fortuna atque condicio quae illorum qui externa bella gesserunt,—quod mihi cum eis vivendum est quos vici ac subegi, isti hostis aut interfectos aut oppressos reliquerunt,—vestrum est, Quirites, si ceteris facta sua recte prosunt, mihi mea ne quando obsint providere. Mentes enim hominum audacissimorum sceleratae ac nefaria ne vobis nocere possent ego providi: ne mihi noceant vestrum est providere.

Cic., in Cat. Or., III.

1. When is *Quirites* used rather than *Romani?*
2. Explain the subjunctive in *possent.*
3. Give the construction of *mihi* and *vestrum.*

III.

Ecce, manus juvenem interea post terga revinctum
Pastores magno ad regem clamore trahebant
Dardanidae, qui se ignotum venientibus ultro,
Hoc ipsum ut strueret Trojamque aperiret Achivis,
Obtulerat, fidens animi, atque in utrumque paratus,
Seu versare dolos, seu certae occumbere morti.

Verg. Aen., Lib. II.

Talibus orabat dictis arasque tenebat,
Cum sic orsa loqui vates: "Sate sanguine divûm,
Tros Anchisiade, facilis descensus Averno;
Noctes atque dies patet atri janua Ditis;
Sed revocare gradum superasque evadere ad auras,
Hoc **opus,** hic labor est."

Id., Lib. VI.

1. What is the subject of the second book of the Aeneid? What of the sixth?
2. When did the author live?
3. Describe the metre. Scan the first line, marking the caesura. Point out any cases of elision in either passage.
4. Explain the derivation of *Dardanidae.* By what other names were the Trojans known?
5. Give the construction of *manus, venientibus, sanguine,* and *noctes.*
6. Explain the subjunctive of *strueret.*

IV.

Caesar, **cum** septimam legionem, quae juxta constiterat, item urgeri ab hoste vidisset, tribunos militum monuit, ut paulatim sese legiones conjungerent, et conversa signa in hostes inferrent. Quo facto, cum alius alii subsidium ferret, neque timerent ne aversi ob hoste circumvenirentur, audacius resistere ac fortius pugnare coeperunt.

Caes. de Bell. Gall., Lib. II.

1. Explain the subjunctive in *conjungerent* and *circumvenirentur.*

V.

Postquam, ut dixi, senatus in Catonis sententiam discessit, consul optumum factu ratus noctem, quae instabat, antecapere, ne quid eo spatio novaretur, triumviros, quae supplicium postulabat, parare jubet: ipse, dispositis praesidiis, Lentulum in carcerem deducit: idem fit ceteris per praetores. Est in carcere locus, quod Tullianum appellatur, **ubi** paullulom ascenderis ad laevam, circiter duodecim pedes humi depressus.

Sall. Cat.

1. Parse *optumum* and *factu.*

Latin Composition.

1. Nothing deters a wise man from obeying the laws of virtue.
2. He says that he was not engaged in the battle.
3. At early dawn, when the top of the mountain was held by Labienus, Considius hastened to

Caesar, with his horse at full speed, and said that the mountain was held by the enemy.

1. Deterreo, sapiens, quominus, parere, lex, virtus.

2. Nego, intersum, proelium.

3. Primus, lux, cum, summus, mons, teneo, accurro, ad, equus, admitto, hostis.

Greek.

[N. B.—Write your name on the top of each page; stating on the first page the amount of Greek read, and the number of lessons studied in Jones's Greek Prose Composition.]

Translate—

Πολὺ δὲ μᾶλλον ὁ Κλέαρχος ἐσπευδεν, ὑποπτεύων μὴ ἀεὶ οὕτω πλήρεις εἶναι τὰς τάφρους ὕδατος· οὐ γὰρ ἦν ὥρα οἵα τὸ πεδίον ἄρδειν· ἀλλ' ἵνα ἤδη πολλὰ προφαίνοιτο τοῖς Ἕλλησι δεινὰ εἰς τὴν πορείαν, τούτου ἕνεκα βασιλέα ὑπώπτευεν ἐπὶ τὸ πεδίον τὸ ὕδωρ ἀφεικέναι. πορευόμενοι δὲ ἀφίκοντο εἰς κώμας, ὅθεν ἀπέδειξαν οἱ ἡγεμόνες λαμβάνειν τὰ ἐπιτήδεια.—ANAB., II. 3.

1. Decline, writing the accent, πορείαν, τάφρους, ὕδωρ, πλήρεις, πολλα. What are the characteristic stem-endings of the three declensions?

2. Synopsis of ἐσπευδεν, εἶναι, ἀφεικέναι. Name the tenses of the Greek verb, with the meaning of each. Separate φαίνοιτο, ἔδειξαν, into their elements. Which modes have special mode-signs? Name the signs. How is the passive voice formed?

3. Composition and literal meaning of ὑποπτεύων, ἀφεικέναι, ἀφίκοντο.

4. Restore the euphony in the following words, giving the rule applicable to each case: ἐλέχθην, ἴδετε, τρίβσω, ἔνπας, ἐτίθμι.

5. Accent the following verb-forms: λιπον, λιπων, λελικως, παυσαι (infin.), λελυμενος.

Translate—

Ἐνθα δὴ προσέρχεται τῷ Ξενοφῶντι τῶν πελταστῶν τις ἀνὴρ Ἀθήνησι φάσκων δεδουλευκέναι, λέγων, ὅτι γιγνώσκοι τὴν φωνὴν τῶν ἀνθρώπων. καὶ οἶμαι, ἔφη, ἐμὴν ταύτην πατρίδα εἶναι· καὶ εἰ μή τι κωλύει, ἐθέλω αὐτοῖς διαλεχθῆναι. ἀλλ' οὐδὲν κωλύει, ἔφη, ἀλλὰ διαλέγου καὶ μάθε πρῶτον, τίνες εἰσίν. οἱ δ' εἶπον ἐρωτήσαντος ὅτι Μάκρωνες.—ANAB., IV. 8.

1. Explain the use of the optative in γιγνώσκοι, and the indicative in κωλύει. State the different ways of expressing condition.

2. Explain the word Ἀθήνησι. How does οἶμαι differ in meaning from οἶδα?

3. In what year was this expedition undertaken? What troops composed the army of Cyrus?

Translate—

"Ἔρχεσθον κλισίην Πηληϊάδεω Ἀχιλῆος·
χειρὸς ἑλόντ' ἀγέμεν Βρισηΐδα καλλιπάρῃον·
εἰ δέ κε μὴ δώῃσιν, ἐγὼ δέ κεν αὐτὸς ἕλωμαι
ἐλθὼν σὺν πλεόνεσσι· τό οἱ καὶ ῥίγιον ἔσται."
Ὣς εἰπὼν προΐει, κρατερὸν δ' ἐπὶ μῦθον ἔτελλεν.
τὼ δ' ἀέκοντε βάτην παρὰ θῖν' ἁλὸς ἀτρυγέτοιο,
Μυρμιδόνων δ' ἐπί τε κλισίας καὶ νῆας ἱκέσθην.
ILIAD, I.

1. Name the metre, and mark the feet and caesura of the first two lines.

2. Attic form of ἀγέμεν, δώῃσιν, πλεόνεσσι, βάτην.

3. Root of προΐει, δώῃσιν, ἐλθόν. Derivation of κρατερόν, ἀέκοντε.

4. Decline ἐγώ, οἱ, ἁλός.

Translate—

"Ὦ φίλοι, Ἀργείων ἡγήτορες ἠδὲ μέδοντες,
εἰ μὲν τις τὸν ὄνειρον Ἀχαιῶν ἄλλος ἔνισπεν,
ψεῦδός κεν φαῖμεν καὶ νοσφιζοίμεθα μᾶλλον·
νῦν δ' ἴδεν ὃς μέγ' ἄριστος Ἀχαιῶν εὔχεται εἶναι.
ἀλλ' ἄγετ', αἴ κέν πως θωρήξομεν υἶας Ἀχαιῶν."
ILIAD, II.

1. Compare μᾶλλον; explain the double λ. Give the suffixes of comparison.

2. Tense and mode of ἔνισπεν, φαῖμεν. Mode of θωρήξομεν; what would be the Attic form used?

3. What Attic form do αἱ κεν represent?

4. What is this dialect called? Name the Greek dialects.

Ancient Geography.

The size and shape of Greece; the principal mountains and rivers; the natural divisions; the political divisions in their order from north to south.

Prose Composition.

It seemed best to us to go to Cyrus. Do not fight with your brother, O Cyrus. If the soldiers arrive this night, the city will not be taken. The general marched rapidly, in order that he might fight as quickly as possible.

INDEX.